NO LONGER
HOPELESS

To Brother
Bill Neece,
Love in Jesus
Dee Keesling

NO LONGER HOPELESS

A True Story of Modern Exorcism

Dee Keesling

Library of Congress Number: 2003092685
ISBN :   Hardcover   1-4134-0700-5
                 Softcover   1-4134-0699-8

This book was printed in the United States of America.

To order additional copies of this book, contact:
Xlibris Corporation
1-888-795-4274
www.Xlibris.com
Orders@Xlibris.com
18842

CONTENTS

Dedicated to Jeni and her determination
for freedom from her entrapments,
and the beautiful person she became-in-Christ.

ACKNOWLEDGMENTS

Honor and praise to the Lord, Jesus Christ for the victory through His shed blood, power, authority and guidance for Jeni's deliverance and healing. Special thanks and appreciation to all who shared in prayer, fasting and in the deliverance services. Thanks also to those who helped edit and put the handwritten manuscript into printed words. Special thanks to my son John, without whom the manuscript would not have been completed.

AUTHOR'S NOTE

This is a true story, inspired by Jeni's victory over her entrapments. Names and details have been changed to maintain the privacy of all involved. All scriptures, unless otherwise noted, are from the New International Version.

PART ONE

JENI'S STORY

CHAPTER 1

Emergency

"Help! Somebody please help!" Ann's eyes were wild with fear as she searched the emergency room for someone, anyone, to help her friend. Jeni merely leaned against her friend with her shoulders hunched inward, wrapped in her own dark misery and only slowly becoming aware of where she was. Ann supported Jeni as best as she could, her knuckle bones gleaming through her skin as she gripped the blood-drenched towel around Jeni's left wrist as firmly as possible. Jeni could feel the pain of Ann's grip, but only as if at a distance. It did not seem to matter, even though she knew as well as Ann that to let the blood flow freely would be disastrous.

Jeni heard Ann sob out loud in terror. The towel was not enough. In a vague haze, Jeni saw Ann's face suddenly go white. She followed her friend's gaze downwards, and saw that her blood had flowed over Ann's hand and was dripping onto the white tiles of the floor.

"Jeni," Ann whispered in horror, "Jeni . . ." Gathering her resolve again, Ann shouted as loudly as she could, stark fear lending even more volume than usual to her voice. "**Help! Help us!**"

The emergency room nurse came out of one of the curtained cubicles, pausing slightly when she saw Jeni's familiar figure. "Oh, Jeni, what have you done to yourself this time?" Seeing the bright red splatters on the floor, her jog broke into a run down the corridor. She snagged a waiting wheelchair along the way, its drag barely slowing her down. "Here," she said to the bedraggled young woman, "Sit here, Jeni."

A piece of human flotsam, Jeni numbly drifted along and did what she was told. She whimpered as she slumped downwards, allowing the wheelchair to catch her weight. Her long blond hair was frazzled and unkempt. It did not matter. Dried blood was crusted on her jeans and sweater. That did not matter, either. The only thing that mattered was trying to keep the emptiness, the pain, at bay. The physical pain of her sliced arm was nothing compared to the pain of her tortured soul. Her perfect facial features contorted into a rictus of agony, mirroring the agony of the wound within herself which could not be so easily stitched as the flesh of her wrist.

"Here we are, Jeni," the nurse said as they approached the examining room. "Come on now. Stand up and let me help you onto the table." Once Ann and Nurse Whitehall had supported and half-lifted her onto the table, the nurse adjusted and re-tightened her grip on Jeni's wrist. Using her other hand, she grabbed up the phone from its hook on the wall. "Dr. Long, you're needed in emergency, **STAT!**" The nurse impatiently waved Ann back out the cubicle. "Go on, now, to the waiting room until she's through."

Turning her attention back to Jeni's arm, Nurse Whitehall shifted her grip slightly, keeping the pressure on Jeni's deeply gouged wrist while she carefully peeled away the towel soaked and sticky with the young woman's blood. The nurse shook her head as she looked down at Jeni's arm. "How many scars will this one make, Jeni?"

Does it matter? It did not matter to Jeni. She did not care. Did anyone? Jeni was pretty certain that Whitehall did not care; her internal antennae detected pure disgust in the nurse's voice. Feeling attacked, Jeni automatically roused to defend herself. "It was an accident this time. I didn't mean to cut so deep," Jeni retorted in a frayed voice.

The nurse's nostrils pinched as her lips hardened. "Don't try to con me, Jeni. I'm going to call your therapist. You just might be admitted to the mental health unit —again."

Jeni shrank inside herself, the momentary anger swamped in yet another rush of fear of judgment and rejection. No one did care, did they. "Please Mrs. Whitehall, it was an accident. Just have the doctor stitch me up and let me go."

"Jeni, if you want help, you need to start by helping yourself. Now, how about beginning by telling me the truth," the nurse insisted.

Tears gathered in the corners of her eyes. "You won't believe me anyway. Nobody believes me. No one even cares about me; I just want to die," the twenty year old whined in despair.

"We do care," countered the nurse, "but we can't help you when you try to hide the truth from us."

Jeni was stung from what remained of her apathy. This was caring? Accusing her? She raised herself up on her right elbow and bellowed with the energy from an upsurge of anger and resentment, "Okay! **Okay!** I did it on purpose! Are you happy to know that?" The brief spurt of anger fizzled out as quickly as it had appeared. Jeni's body slumped back onto the cold hard table and her face crumpled back into lines of despair. Choking back a sob, she softly added, "But I didn't mean to cut myself so deep. Honest, I didn't. You have to believe me."

*   *   *

The day had begun with the early darkness of winter staring back at Jeni as she gazed sightlessly out of her bedroom window. Empty darkness. Everywhere.

All day and through the evening Jeni had been struggling against the voices from her past . . . accusatory voices, taunting voices, voices filled with disgust for her. She was nothing and no one. These were not the voices of hallucination; worse, these were the voices embedded in her own memory, and as such she could not dispel them as lies or illusions.

No good, no good. Not good for anything. Not worth caring about. *Quit yer crying. If you were a good girl and did what you were told without makin' such a fuss, it wouldn't hav'ta hurt at all.*

Wouldn't hav'ta hurt at all. . . . Jeni absently twiddled the razor blade in her hand. *If you were a good girl . . . not hurt at all.* . . . Somewhere deep inside Jeni there was a fragmentary, foggy concept; if only somehow she could make this pain deep inside her soul visible on the outside, somehow there might be a way to heal it. Either way, even being dead had to be better than living like this.

"Jeni!" Ann stood frozen in the bedroom doorway. "**Jeni!**" Ann disappeared and Jeni wondered vaguely what her roommate had been yelling about. Ann careened back through the doorway, a towel flapping from her hand. "Give me your arm!" Ann's voice shook. Jeni shrugged then held out her right arm. Ann snatched the blood-tinged razor away, then reached for Jeni's left arm. "Give it to me, Jeni!" Jeni looked up at Ann's face, the muscles tight and rigid. Then she looked down at her own wrist.

Blood was pouring from the deep gash she had made. Funny. It did not seem to hurt like it should have, considering how much blood there was. She watched, distant and uninvolved, as Ann grabbed her wrist and wrapped the towel around it, putting as much pressure against the wound as possible. Jeni roused herself enough to say, "Don't worry, Ann. It doesn't matter."

Ann's eyes grew even wider in her shock. "Don't you dare say it doesn't matter! You could be bleeding to death right now! Get up! **Get up!** I'm taking you to the hospital." Jeni did not want to argue. It did not matter that much. She got up.

Ann's grip on the towel slipped for an instant, and both of them could see how quickly the stain on the terry cloth was spreading. "Come on, Jeni. Now!" Ann tugged her friend through the apartment door and down the stairs to the outside. The hospital was only a short block away; Ann pulled Jeni out into the darkness. "Hurry, Jeni!"

The night's freezing wind seemed to coat Jeni's face in a layer of ice, making it nearly as numb as she was inside. The wind stingingly whipped the ends of her hair into her eyes, but Jeni really could not be bothered to notice. It did not matter. Nothing mattered. "Come on, Jeni, just a little further." Ann's voice seemed to reach her from a great distance. "Jeni . . . . Jeni!" Jeni leaned on her friend and allowed herself to be pulled forward. She did not care, it was just easier.

A tear slid downward, hastened on its way by the freezing wind. She did care, but Jeni tried not to admit it. To admit that she cared was to admit to the pain . . . . the pain . . . . the pain that she could never seem to get away from. No matter what she tried.

"Jeni!" The lights of the hospital's emergency entrance threw the taut lines of strain on Ann's face into a glaring relief of highlights and shadows. "Jeni, come on now. Let's get out of the cold. Come on." Ann pulled her further into the hospital, trying to keep a firm grip on Jeni's arm.

*   *   *

And now, here she was in the ER, waiting for a doctor to sew her back up. Her chest was still heaving with barely suppressed sobs when Dr. Long entered the curtained cubicle. With only a glance, he shook his head and sighed. "Well, I see you have given us a reason to add another page to your already bulging medical record, young lady."

Jeni shrank from his impatient tone. She needed him to care about her . . . . She needed **someone** to care about her. To prove to her that she was worth being cared about. As he stitched and bandaged her wrist, she pleaded, "Please don't be angry with me. I try, really I do."

"If you were trying, then why didn't you pick up the phone and call your psychologist instead of picking up the razor blade?" Dr. Long shook his head in frustration as he bent over this latest self-inflicted wound and carefully stitched the layers back together.

Jeni could not face his question, so she pretended not to have heard it. Instead, she focused on watching him pull off the latex gloves and throw them in the disposal bin. But the fear would not leave her. The fear that he was angry. The fear that he would turn away. "Are you mad at me?"

She was not reassured when he apparently ignored her question, picking up her chart and beginning to write his notes in it. The fear rose higher, sharper. "Are you going to put me in lockup again?" To be in lockup meant that she was rejectable . . . had in fact been rejected as being a fit part of society.

He raised his eyebrows and looked at her over his glasses. "What do you think I should do?"

"Please let me go home," she begged. Silently she thought to herself, *Nobody understands. Nobody!*

He looked at her for a long moment, his thoughts hidden, before he turned to Nurse Whitehall. "I'm finished here. She's all yours now." Without another glance, he brusquely clipped his pen into his pocket then strode out of the room and on his way to see his next patient. With a sigh and a slight shake of the head, the nurse gently helped Jeni to her feet.

Unnerved by Dr. Long's silence, Jeni's fear flashed into anger again for a moment. She turned on Nurse Whitehall. "Why don't you just let me die and do **everyone** a favor?" If she were dead, then it would not matter anymore that no one was there who cared. She would no longer have to see them not caring. If she were dead, would the pain stop?

The curtain to the emergency room cubicle was pulled back long enough for Jeni's therapist to enter. Jeni looked up at the motion, her blue eyes wide and her vision blurred. When she saw who it was, a raw breath caught in Jeni's throat and she tried to stifle the tears. *If anyone can help me, Carol can. She understands me better than anyone else in this crummy world,* Jeni thought. A dim glimmer of hope slowly pushed its way through the gloomy darkness that enshrouded her.

Carol was a psychologist who really cared about her clients. They were not just case numbers and file folders to Carol; her warmth and sensitivity for her clients was obvious to them and to others. The therapist looked over at Jeni, who's head had dropped again. She then glanced at the nurse, who merely shook her head and rolled her eyes upward. Carol moved close enough so that Jeni could feel the warmth of her presence, but not so close that she would feel crowded. With a deep sense of relief, Jeni listened to Carol's calm voice reach out to her, gentle as fingers stroking the soft down of a kitten's fur. "I heard that you needed to see me, Jeni."

The young woman stood motionless at the side of the examining table, afraid but without knowing what exactly it was she feared. Her shoulders drew further inward and the cascading hair surrounded the bent head, hiding the troubled eyes that stared at the floor. Jeni was so relieved that Carol had come. She wanted to say, 'Thanks for coming. I am so sorry for cutting myself again. Please don't be angry. Help me, please, help me.' But the words caught in her throat. She could not get a single word past the tightness that threatened to overwhelm her again. She longed for the warmth and calm gentleness in Carol's voice, but it was almost as if she were afraid of it, too.

As Jeni tentatively walked forward a pace, Carol pushed back the curtain that had given a semblance of privacy for Jeni in the little emergency room cubicle. Her voice was gentle, calm and reassuring. "Come along Jeni, we can talk in my office." Jeni tucked her head in further towards her collar bone. She still felt alone but knew that Carol was there. She could feel Carol's warm presence acting as a bulwark against the darkness that had overwhelmed her earlier that night. If only Jeni could feel so calm herself. If only she could be so strong, even in the face of the darkness.

The two women walked in silence down the nearly empty hospital corridors, heading toward the mental health suite that housed Carol's office. Jeni could feel the support she drew simply from being in Carol's presence. As they walked, Jeni's mind spun a repetitive silent word wheel. *She came! She cares! Somebody **does** care for me and it's Carol. I know she does. She really cares.* Being with Carol, she could almost believe that she was worth caring about. Jeni had hit rock bottom, but maybe she could look to Carol to help her get back up. *Thank you, Carol. Thank you. You are a friend, a real friend. You give me so much hope! Maybe I am worth caring about, after all. Or at least, maybe I will be someday.* Again, the words were choked off in her constricted throat. *Will I ever be able to tell her how much she's helped me? Why can't I tell her?*

CHAPTER 2

Drugs

C arol unlocked her office door, pulled it open and motioned Jeni inside. Jeni gently cradled her injured wrist as she slouched across the room, passing Carol's desk on the way to the familiar, comfortable upholstered high back chair. She did not look at the desk. She did not have to. She already knew that there would be a thick file folder with her name on it sitting there. Heaving a sigh, Jeni gratefully sank into the chair and squirmed slightly to settle into the most comfortable position. Carol followed, closing the door for privacy before taking the other upholstered chair. She sat near, but not too close, and waited. Jeni knew that Carol would give her some time to gather herself, collect her thoughts and to express what was on her mind. The young woman looked off to the side. She knew that her therapist was waiting for her to explain what had happened tonight. She knew Carol wanted and needed to know what had triggered this latest incident of acting out.

Jeni pulled her cigarettes and lighter from her blue jeans' pocket. She could not talk about it yet. She concentrated on lighting up the smoke. She sucked in a long draw, and then exhaled while the smoke encircled her before dissipating into the atmosphere. "I needed that," she whispered and then shivered. "I haven't had a drag for three hours." Jeni continued to focus on the glowing end of her cigarette. If only she could drop away into the cigarette's embers and come up somewhere else. Somewhere far away from probing questions that acted as mirrors. Minutes passed.

Carol broke the silence "Would you like to tell me what happened before you cut your wrist tonight?"

Jeni's face clouded. She knew how important it was for her to share her feelings with Carol. But how do you explain what you yourself do not understand? She trusted her psychologist implicitly, but it was embarrassingly hard to verbalize even what she did know. She finally mustered up the courage to ask, "Are you mad at me?"

"No, I am not mad at you," Carol responded patiently as she continued to watch Jeni's body language. Jeni scuffed her feet against the rug and intermittently squirmed like a child sitting in the principal's office. She looked out the window into the night. She looked at the plant in the corner. She hunched her shoulders for a moment and stared back into the embers of her cigarette.

After another deep drag on her cigarette, Jeni bent her head slightly, gathered her courage and looked up at Carol. "I didn't mean to cut so deep, honest," Jeni offered. "It really did scare me when it bled so much!." Jeni's eyes dropped again. "Why do I do this to myself?"

"Could it be for attention?" Carol suggested.

"No way!" Jeni's eyebrows furled. She did not act out for attention, but at the same time she did know deep down that it was a cry for help. This kind of thing always happened when her depression and anxieties became too intense for her to take any more. When the pain became more than she could handle.

Using the embers of her glowing cigarette butt to light another one, Jeni puffed as she tried to use the calming rhythm to quiet the turmoil and confusion within. Eventually, though, the only thing the passing of time accomplished was the burning of tobacco.

Jeni looked over and saw that Carol was watching her. Carol had to get her client to talk before she could help her to resolve the deep troubling issues. Jeni winced slightly when her therapist lifted the bulging file folder from the desk. "I see here in your file that you called an ambulance last week for your friend, Ann. She had overdosed, right?"

Jeni's head jerked upright. "Yeah." She looked at Carol with disconcerted eyes. "Why bring that up?"

Carol leafed through some of the pages of the file before looking back up. Her eyes held Jeni's. "I bring it up because there is a pattern here. One perhaps you may not even be aware of." Carol's forefinger flicked against the manila folder. "Your records say that you've been having a lot more problems and crises since Ann has moved into your apartment. That indicates to me that there is some kind of a problem occurring." Carol continued to hold Jeni's eyes. "Now, you probably know better than I do what that problem is." She waited for a moment, but Jeni just stared back with widened eyes. "Since you have already told me that Ann abuses drugs, it makes me wonder if you are doing drugs, too."

"Oooh," Jeni cringed, noticeably straining deeper into the chair. She did not realize that others could recognize the change in her lifestyle. "I don't use them as much as Ann does," she cried in a vain attempt to justify herself.

Carol lifted her eyebrows. "But that wasn't the question, was it Jeni?" Carol closed the file folder and returned it to her desk. "Something has been causing you to have more problems since Ann moved into your apartment. It sounds like you have a pretty good idea what that problem might be. The question is, what are you willing to do to help yourself?"

More painful silence ensued as Jeni reflected on the significant changes in her life since Ann had moved in with her. *I was already drinking a lot, but Carol's right about the drugs . . . they started after we'd begun sharing the apartment. Yeah,* she smiled slightly to herself, *we've had some pretty wild parties at our place.* The faint smile quickly disappeared as her reverie continued. *Pot, coke, crack, heroin, ecstacy . . . you name it, we've tried it. I have to admit, we have had some real bummers too.* However, she was not ready to admit all of that to Carol. Instead she offered a defense. "If you had horrible nightmares like I have, you would be glad to have someone there too. You might say that I need her."

"Maybe," Carol replied. "Have the nightmares slacked off?"

"No, not really," Jeni sighed. "If anything they're worse and more frequent."

"Exactly, Jeni. The nightmares are symptoms of distress. The same thing is true of the slashing of your wrist tonight." Carol shifted slightly in her chair. "Jeni, you do know that using drugs makes all sorts of health and mental health problems worse, don't you? Many people use them for escape, but what kind of escape is it that only makes the problems get bigger?"

Jeni looked down at her bandaged wrist cradled carefully in her lap. What she was hearing did make a lot of sense. "Carol, um, it isn't just the nightmares. The blank outs are getting worse and happening more often, too." Jeni used the term 'blank out' to refer to the time lapses of which she had no memory. Sometimes they lasted a few hours, other times for days. She did not lose consciousness during these lapses; she walked, talked and acted as if she were fully aware of what was happening but would not remember any of it.

"Carol, do you remember when the doctor put me on dilantin to try and stop the blank outs? He told me they might be caused by epilepsy."

"Do you still believe that the dilantin did not help?" Carol inquired.

"No, it didn't help. Nothing changed when I took it; nothing changed after I stopped. I have not taken any medication for the blank outs for a very long time." Jeni's stomach knotted slightly as she thought for a moment. "Carol," Jeni said pensively. "I saw the true story of a college student on TV, and she came down with schizophrenia. She had blank out periods where she also couldn't remember. Am I schizophrenic?" Jeni suppressed a shudder. That poor girl had some really difficult problems to deal with.

"No, you're not." Carol assured her patient.

Jeni was not reassured, though. "Shouldn't I know my diagnosis in case I'm taken someplace else during an emergency," Jeni prodded.

This time it was Carol who took her time answering. "You do not have schizophrenia, you have what we call a personality disorder."

"Oh, that's a relief." Jeni smiled and snuffed out another cigarette butt. As she played with the crushed butt in the ashtray, Carol stood, signalling that the session was ending.

"Jeni, I want you to spend time this week looking at your current lifestyle and circumstances. I want you to decide whether or not your present situation is helping you, or hurting you." Carol gave Jeni a warm smile. "I think that you have a much better idea now of what might be causing the recent upsurge in problems."

Jeni followed her to the door. "Yeah," she said thoughtfully as she paused in the doorway. Then she lifted her eyes up and gave her therapist a smile. "Carol, you've given me several things to think about. Thanks for being here and for not sending me to lockup." Carols eyes smiled back, and Jeni turned and walked down the corridor. She still cradled her left arm, but her back was straighter. Her shoulders no longer sagged. Much calmer now, Jeni left the hospital more determined to have better control over her life and actions. *I can always count on Carol to help me see things better*, she thought with a renewed vigor in her step.

*   *   *

Through the night, Jeni thought about what Carol had said. Her arm acted as an aching reminder of how badly things had been getting away from her lately. *You know, she's right,* she thought to herself the next morning over coffee. *The drugs have got to go.* Curled up in her big overstuffed easy chair, Jeni worked to remember the twelve steps of the Alcoholics Anonymus program. She had learned them as a kid when one of her friend's relatives had gone off the booze, and she was pretty certain that they would help her now.

Even with a firm decision and leaning on the support of the twelve steps, the next few days were not easy for Jeni as she strived to stop using the drugs. Ann could not or would not understand that she was serious. Jeni sighed; it was especially hard when she watched Ann snort right there in her apartment. It was even harder when Ann offered to share her drugs with Jeni, encouraging and even prodding Jeni to join in.

To make the change even more difficult, all of her friends got high as a matter of course. That was just what they did whenever they were hanging out. Jeni had thought about it, and at first was sure it would not matter much if she stayed away from the drugs. They were her friends, right? And a friend should still like you even if you did not want to share a joint with them. Jeni was confident that it would work itself out.

Only a few hours after having thought all that through, Jeni answered the ringing of the telephone. "Jen, how ya doin', babe? Do you s'pose we can get together this evening?"

"What do you have in mind, Doug?"

"Well," he responded, "Kevin's gonna have the gang in to party at his place tonight. It's a come early, stay late deal. How about meeting me there?"

"Um, well, Doug," Jeni stammered, "can't we go to a movie?"

"If you want to, Jen. I'll tell Kevin that we'll be late."

Jeni sighed. "Doug, I *don't* want to party!"

"I can't believe what I'm hearin'," Doug replied, more than

a little irritated. "I'm goin' to party tonight whether or not you go."

Jeni was torn. She liked Doug. He was so-o-o-o good looking, and besides, she craved everything that would be at the party. Not just the drugs, but the feeling of being a part of a group and being accepted. She wanted to go so much and yet she knew that it would be a mistake. Slowly and reluctantly, she forced the words out. "Go without me then. I don't want to party any more."

"Have it your way, baby," Doug said sharply. The click of the phone being hung up reverberated in Jeni's ears.

At first she thought maybe it was just Doug. Over the next few days, however, she found out that every guy who called her for a date was not really looking to spend time with her, Jeni, the person . . . they were only interested in a girl to party and get high with. Pounding a pillow soggy with tears, she vented her frustration and pain at night, determined that she would not give in. If all they were interested in was another body to do the drugs with, then maybe they were not really her friends after all. Maybe you really could not care about drugs and about another person at the same time. Jeni sobbed. Why did doing the right thing have to be so hard?

*   *   *

A few nights after Doug's call, Ann was clearing the supper table while Jeni began washing the dishes. "Hey Jeni, our welfare checks will be in the mail this week. How about throwing a party?"

Jeni bit her lower lip. "Ann, I've already told you I am trying to quit the drugs."

"Quit the drugs!" Ann scoffed. "I know that's what you said a few days ago, but I thought you'd have gotten over yourself by now. What's the deal? Have you lost your mind?"

Ann's sarcasm and acid tone caused Jeni to cringe on the inside, but she was able to keep her eyes and voice level on the outside. "No, but I am afraid I might if I don't change my lifestyle."

"Oh Jeni, get off it." Ann replied in disgust. "We might as well get some fun out of life while we can."

"That's just it Ann. When I think of the trouble the drugs have gotten me into, they just don't seem so great anymore."

Her own eyes narrowing, Ann stopped in her tracks, put her hands on her hips and glared straight into her roommate's eyes. "You are crazy." Her nostrils flared. "What are you trying to do, get me to buy all the drugs?"

Jeni ignored that question. "Just think about what happened to Ron and Maria's baby," she said. Inside she was pleading for Ann to understand. "Little Bobby was born deformed and died a newborn, because they were druggies."

Ann gasped, but quickly recovered. "That was their bad luck. I'm not going to let it stop me from enjoying my life."

Inside, Jeni sighed. Ann would not understand. She was not sure if Ann would ever understand. Jeni felt old. "That's up to you, of course," Jeni said, "but I have decided not to have anymore parties in my apartment."

"Your apartment? Okay, you can have **your** apartment all to yourself!" Ann screamed as she stormed out of the kitchen.

Within twenty-four hours, Ann had found someone else to bunk with, had bagged her clothes and left. Jeni did miss her at first, but was compensated by her regained independence and privacy. Not having others around her popping pills and snorting coke did help her in the struggle to leave behind the chemical dependency. The storm really had been worth it.

CHAPTER 3

Dabbling in Witchcraft

The summer sunshine was streaming in through the window when Carol looked up from the papers on her desk. Her eyebrows rose slightly in surprise to see Jeni already standing in her open doorway; she was unexpectedly early for her appointment. "Come on in and have a seat. Give me a minute or so to put this stuff away. You're a little early for this week's session." Carol smiled.

"A little early," Jeni replied as she slipped across the room and dropped into the familiar chair. She glanced at Carol a couple of times, but quickly dropped her head when Carol glanced up at her. The therapist rapidly gathered several sheets together, closed the folder and dropped it into a drawer.

"That can all wait until later. What's on your mind, Jeni? Has something this past week bothered you?" Carol asked.

"Well, yes . . . sort of." Jeni took a deep breath. It was a push to begin telling Carol how disturbed she was about the movie she had seen earlier in the week. "Have you seen 'The Exorcist'?"

"Did you see it?" Carol prodded.

"Yes," Jeni said slowly with a shudder, "and it was gruesome. That kid played with a ouija board. I did, too, at youth camp one year." Jeni paused in thought. "Boy, that was a fiasco." The memories rose and caught at Jeni, pulling her down into themselves.

*   *   *

She was just a kid again, back at the youth camp for sick teens that she had gone to one summer. She was fascinated with the ouija board board that one of the boys had brought. After a while of watching, he had even let her put her fingers on the small board they called a planchette.

The question she asked the ouija board was, "Why am I sick so much?" The planchette slowly moved to the letter "L", then it went to the "U", followed by a "P" and then another "U" before stopping on "S".

Jeni was startled. Her diagnosis was lupus. The kids started chiding her . . ."You made it move".

Her eyebrows furrowed. "No, I didn't."

"Come on, Jeni. Tell the truth."

Jeni's eyes grew wider as she defended herself. "It moved itself," she insisted.

"You're a liar, too," one kid accused. Then Jeni heard the chorus "liar . . . liar . . . liar" as the rest of the kids took up the litany.

She felt the prickling of the tears as they gathered behind her eyes. Instead of giving in to them, she fought the tears as she stood to leave. Struggling to keep her mouth from trembling, she declared loudly, "It did too. It moved itself. It did. It did."

She quickly ran down the cabin's steps before the others could see the tears that she could no longer hold back.

*   *   *

"Jeni." Jeni blinked at the sound of her name. Even now, years later in Carol's office, the laughter that she had heard behind her then was haunting her once again.

Carol had waited patiently. She had seen that Jeni was dealing with something within herself, but now it was time to get her to talk about it outside of herself. "Jeni, I need you to tell me about it."

Finally, Jeni was able to express her reaction to the ouija board. "It was weird," she said with a slight shiver. "We put our hands on this wooden thing. Then asked it questions and it went all over the board, from letter to letter, spelling out the answers. Some of the kids got disgusted and said we were making it spell those things. I know I didn't push it . . . it just moved itself around the board and spelled out the answers to the questions we had asked it. Honest!"

"So, your experience with the ouija board was rather startling, I take it."

Jeni pulled out a cigarette and lit up. There were times when the nicotine really helped steady her. "It was more than just that, though, you know." Jeni drew in a deep lung-full. "There was also this time in high school . . . . It got a lot more serious than just words spelled out on a wooden plank." She closed her eyes against the memory, only to have it flood the darkness behind her eyelids.

*   *   *

She was standing at her locker, looking over the reading list for her English class. She had to choose one of these books, but had no idea which one might be most interesting.

"Hey, Jeni," Tom said as he draped an arm over her locker

door. "What's up?"

Jeni looked up and smiled. "Not much, other than trying to figure out which of these books might be the least boring," she answered with a laugh.

"You like to babysit, don't you? You might enjoy number ten on the list; it's about a kid."

She ran her fingers down the list to book number ten. "That does look interesting. Thanks, Tom. I think I probably will do my report on that one." He smiled and sauntered on down the hall.

During study hall, Jeni went down to the library and checked the book out. It was no time at all before she was reading and growing more engrossed in the story line. When it began to include some occult practices, she was even more intrigued.

Seeing Tom at school the next day she skipped forward a couple of steps to catch up with him. Holding the book up for him to see, she exclaimed, "Thanks again, Tom. This is going to make a great book report. I mean, it's really interesting; the main characters are into occult stuff."

"What kind of stuff?" he asked, interested.

"They cast spells on people and read tarot cards. I'm anxious to finish reading it to see what other weird stuff they get into."

A few days later her mother called to her through the house. "Jeni, telephone. It's Tom."

Jeni took the receiver. "Hi Tom, what's up?"

"I was telling some of the guys about the book you're reading and we've checked out some other books on the subject. How about meeting us a little early at the church before the youth meeting?"

"Okay," Jeni agreed. "I'll go to the church about an hour early." She put the handset down and went back to her reading. She was getting closer to the end and was pushing to get it finished as soon as possible, even though the things she was reading about were truly awful. She did not have much choice.

She had to hand in her report by the next Monday's class; there was no time for her to start over with a different book.

Sunday came quickly and Jeni arrived at the church early as planned. Tom and several other youth were already there. All went to the Sunday school room, chatting on the way. Rick was the most vocal. "This could be more fun than a great video game. Virginia, did you remember the tarot cards?"

"Got 'em," Virginia said as she pulled them out of her pocket and set them on the table. The group seated themselves around the table. There was some giggling and some ribbing as Rick made a stab at telling each one's fortune. Jeni could see Virginia put the tarot cards back in her pocket, but then her memory skipped forward. What had started out as just fun and games was getting serious and foul . . . just like it had in the book she had read.

Rick was now standing next to the table with a curl to his lip. "What teacher do you hate the most?" His eyes challenged his peers. They looked at each other and then back to Rick. "How about old lady Towser?"

Jeni interrupted him. "Where is this going, Rick?"

"Doesn't she downright bug everybody?" he continued. There were no verbal responses, but the other kids stirred in their chairs and scuffed their feet on the floor. The sudden note of vindictiveness in Rick's voice made all of them nervous. Rick told them, "We can get even with Towser by casting a spell on her."

Jeni suddenly felt nauseated. She jumped to her feet and squared off on Rick. "Stop it. Stop it right now! This is not a video game. This is evil. **Evil**, do you hear me?!"

Jeni turned her sickened eyes on the other kids at the table. "The occult may look like fun at first, but not for long. The more I read in my book, the worse things got. It's a trap! It ruins lives! It's one thing to hurt ourselves but much worse to hurt others. Things I learned near the end of the book were just awful! Horrible! There was even killing of little kids and babies for rituals."

Everyone's eyes were on Jeni as she bared her feelings. "I was intrigued about this stuff and wanted to know more about it. I've had enough." Silent and still, they watched as she flung herself out the door into the hallway. Scant moments later the outside doors crashed with the force of her passing.

*   *   *

"Jeni." The psychologist's voice broke into her reverie. "What happened in high school?"

Slowly and softly Jeni spoke, "The movie reminded me of a book that I had read in high school. Of all the books listed on the prospective reading list, there was one that looked interesting to me. And boy was it ever!"

Jeni's face became more animated as she shared with Carol her intrigue with the introduction she received on the occult from this book. "Some of my friends got more books on this subject from the library, so we could explore it further."

"What do you mean by 'explore'?"

"One fellow used tarot cards to tell our fortunes, oh, and we tried to cast some spells. At first it was just like a game." Jeni's voice began to slow down as her shoulders suddenly drooped. "Some of the kids said there was a little levitation when we tried it, but I couldn't tell."

"Is there a reason why you are telling me these things?" Carol inquired.

Tears welled up in Jeni's eyes. "It ended up getting really nasty. One of the guys wanted to put a curse on one of our teachers. It was just so . . . mean . . . . so ugly." Jeni looked down at her hands. "I think the whole thing kind of messed me up. I know the movie did. Some people say that the movie was inspired by a true story and that the ouija board messed that kid up." Her eyes glistening with unshed moisture, she looked up at Carol. "Actually, I'm glad I backed off from that occult stuff when I did. I think . . . I think that maybe there really is such a thing as evil. What do you think?"

"Since it struck you as being evil and it disturbs you, I think that you would be very wise to stay away from it," Carol said. "As they say, why borrow trouble?" Carol smiled over at her client. "You do some good thinking, Jeni."

CHAPTER 4

Campus Catastrophe

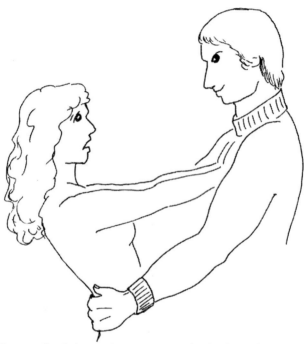

J eni walked down the noisy corridor looking for her assigned
dorm room, her suitcases banging against her hips. Deciding
to give up her apartment and start college had been a big step for
Jeni; listening to the cheerful chatter in the hall, she was glad that
she had. College could open up a whole new world for her. She
smiled to herself as she continued checking the numbers on the
doors. Ah! There it was. She had finally found Rm. 205.

Maneuvering herself and her luggage through the door was
almost like a comedy routine; finally she sidled in sideways with
only a few knocks against her shins. It was a distinct pleasure to set

her heavy suitcases down beside the empty bed. With a heartfelt sigh of relief she straightened her back.

A feminine voice off to her left chuckled. "Those stairs are a killer, all right. Hi, I guess you're my new roommate," said the busy brunette as she was putting her clothes in the dresser drawer. She paused long enough to smile and lift a hand in greeting to Jeni. "My name is Rosalyn, and your's is . . . ?"

"I'm Jeni. It's good to meet you."

"I left these drawers free for you, okay?" Rosalyn pulled open the closet door. "And although there isn't much space in here, I think we can manage." Her eyes crinkled at the corners as she smiled.

Jeni grinned back, feeling welcomed and wanted. "That will do just fine for me. Thanks."

The two young women quickly felt at ease with one another. Both were freshman and they soon discovered that they would be in most of their classes together. It was not long before they began to tell each other about their interests and even share some confidences with one another. Within just a few days their relationship had bonded into a strong friendship.

Jeni made other friends as well; the young men were especially quick to notice her arrival on campus. She was a beauty with her long golden hair and slim figure and it took very little time before she began being asked out on dates. The fall whirled past, and Jeni felt happy. Classes were going well, she had made new friends, and even the past was leaving her alone for the moment. Life seemed to be making sense and she felt a new sense of purpose and accomplishment. She was doing something to help herself and giving her life a direction. She was certain that she would be able to pull her life together now.

As their first semester was nearing its end, Rosalyn was reading the campus newspaper. "Jeni, listen to this: 'furnished apartment in house bordering the campus. Call 555-3875'."

Jeni looked up from a textbook, smiling. "That's interesting. Let's check it out." She reached for the phone and dialed. Before the day was over, the two of them had put a deposit on the apartment. Before the month was over, the semester had ended.

Chattering, laughing and happy, the two moved their belongings into their new flat. They loved their new home. Unlike the dorm rooms, this place felt like it was theirs . . . like it was home.

In no time at all, the new semester began and Jeni's social life picked right back up where it had left off. If anything, Jeni was getting asked out for dates more now than she had before. She thought she should be happy that she seemed to be so popular, but she was not. She really did not understand why, but lately she was getting more and more depressed and feeling more and more out of control of herself and her life. Jeni herself did not notice that her despondency grew worse after she had gone out with certain fellows. She did not realize just how much she was withdrawing from other people, either. Rosalyn noticed, though, and the change in her warm, outgoing friend gave her a great deal of concern.

Finally, one night Jeni came home looking as brittle and fragile as glass and as if she would shatter at the least vibration. Rosalyn decided that she had to at least try and help, even though she did not know how. "Is something wrong," Rosalyn asked, her concern reaching out through her voice.

Jeni stopped immediately and stood there. For a long moment she stood perfectly still and Rosalyn waited, hoping that Jeni would open the door. Jeni tried to; she tried to find the words somewhere inside herself, but all she found was pain. "Can't talk about it," Jeni responded softly, defeated in her hunt for the words. Quietly, she walked away.

During the next few weeks Rosalyn was awakened several times by Jeni's moans and screams. Jeni had said she sometimes had nightmares, but Rosalyn had never seen anyone thrash like that in their sleep before. It was frightening. At the same time, Jeni's gloom and depression increased as time passed. There were also the flares of sullenness and irritability. And it did not stop there. There were occasions, sometimes even days, when Jeni changed from being her normal, really nice self into someone vicious and mean. Rosalyn wondered what had happened to the person she had met the Fall before; at times it was almost as if Jeni were a different person.

One night when Jeni returned from a date, Rosalyn could

practically feel the dark cloud following Jeni when she came into their bedroom. Rosalyn sat up in bed and ached for Jeni. She could barely stand to see her friend like this. What was wrong? "Jeni, I'm really worried about you. Is there anything at all I can do to cheer you up a little?" Jeni's head dropped and she wrung her hands, finding it difficult to speak. Rosalyn waited many long minutes, slumping further and further back onto her pillow as the time went past.

Rosalyn was almost asleep when Jeni spoke, oh so softly. "May I ask you something?"

Roused by the soft sound but uncertain, Rosalyn raised her head to look. Jeni was still sitting, almost cringing, on the side of her bed. "Oh Jeni!" Rosalyn threw back her covers and ran over to her friend's bed, her face crumpled with her concern for her friend and her compassion for Jeni's obvious pain. Rosalyn sat down close beside her and took Jeni's hands into her own. "Oh, Jeni, what's wrong?"

Jeni's eyes squeezed tightly shut for a moment. Her throat was tight with unshed tears and it was hard to force the words out between her clenched jaws. But she had to know. She could trust Rosalyn to tell her the truth, and she had to know. After a brief pause and with difficulty, Jeni pushed her question out into the open air. "Do your boyfriends expect you to have sex every time you go out?"

Rosalyn strained to hear Jeni's soft, unstable voice. Not entirely certain that she had heard her friend right, she asked, "Do they expect sex?"

Jeni nodded, then broke into sobs. Rosalyn put her arms around her friend until the sobbing stopped. When Jeni had calmed slightly, Rosalyn answered her. "Oh Jeni, no. The boys I go out with know that I won't have sex with them. I've told them that. No sex until marriage; I'm a virgin and plan to stay that way until I get married."

Jeni emphatically declared, "I hate it!" Her hands balled into fists, the nails digging into her own flesh. "I hate it!" and fresh, scalding tears coursed down her face.

"Sex?" Rosalyn asked.

Jeni shuddered. "Yes. I hate it."

Rosalyn reached out with all her might to try to understand and help her friend. "Jeni, why do you have sex if you hate it? Girl, you're gorgeous. You're fun to be with. You are a genuinely nice person. You don't have to resort to sex to attract guys."

"Really?" The forlorn question in Jeni's voice nearly broke Rosalyn's heart.

"Really," Rosalyn reiterated firmly. "Just say, **no!**"

"You mean that I don't have to give a guy sex if he asks for it?"

Rosalyn was shocked, but kept it out of her face and voice. She hugged her friend tight. "No, Jeni. You don't have to give anyone anything like that unless, and **until**, you want to. You don't owe them a thing."

Jeni frowned as she absorbed this. "But . . . Rosalyn, they've told me that since I let them take me to dinner or a movie or something, that I do owe them. That I led them to expect something in return." Rosalyn's arms tightened for a moment around Jeni, and Jeni cringed. "Are you mad at me, Rosalyn?"

"Oh kitten, absolutely not! But I *am* absolutely furious that these fellows have lied to you like that! Everything they've told you like that is a lie. They decided to take you out; there should never be strings attached to that!"

Rosalyn took her friend's tear-streaked face between her hands, holding Jeni's eyes with her own. "Jeni," Rosalyn said, "I'm serious. You don't owe them a thing. And Jeni, just tell them *no!*"

This time it was Jeni who gave the big hug. After leaning against her friend for a long moment, Jeni pulled back and smiled weakly into Rosalyn's eyes. "Oh thank you, Rosalyn! I can do that. That's such a relief. I'm going to follow your suggestion and just say no." Jeni's tension melted away.

That night was the first time in more than a month that Jeni was able to sleep through the night without being awakened in the cold sweat aftermath of a nightmare. Her new-found stability would last for almost a week.

*   *   *

The players puffed and panted for a moment. Football season was over, but some of the guys could never get enough. They had a pickup game going, even though there was a foot of snow on the ground. At the end of a play one of the guys looked up, then said with a smirk, "Hey, here comes one."

Looking over, the fullback on the college football team grinned. "Yeah. I do believe that's Jen over there, coming this way."

"You got that right, Mike," the quarterback agreed. He leered at his teammates. "I had a date with her last month and she was easy. All I had to do was sweet talk her a little bit and put her to bed. No resistance, man." He turned to the center for the team and poked him in the ribs none to gently. "Hey Derrick you're still a virgin, aren't you?" Other members of the team snorted with laughter. "What's up with that? Are you chicken?" He turned and looked at the other guys. "Or maybe it's that you don't like girls."

Derrick's face turned red and his neck swelled like a bull's. "I ain't chicken and I like girls just fine."

"Yeah," the quarterback sneered. "Prove it."

Derrick glared, then turned with a hulking motion of his shoulders. Taking a better look at the girl walking towards them down the sidewalk, he did have to agree. The guys were right. She was a looker. As Jeni approached, Derrick called out to her, "What brings you out, sweet stuff?"

"Hi guys. I 've been studying so much my brain is on overload. I decided some fresh air and a brisk walk would do me some good." She kicked at the snow beside the sidewalk. "At least I hope that the cold knocks some of those cobwebs out." She looked up and smiled.

Mike bumped Derrick's shoulder, trying to nudge him into action. Derrick looked back with a glare and a shove of his own. Nevertheless, the bait was taken. "Hey, listen, have you seen the new movie that's playing down the road yet?" he asked.

"Not yet," Jeni answered.

"How about this evening? Want to go see it with me?" Derrick asked. There was a little sniggering, but most of the fellows were just bobbing their heads up and down and smirking at each other. They were already looking forward to hearing all about it.

*   *   *

It was a good movie, kind of romantic, but with enough action that Derrick enjoyed it, too. Jeni hated to see it come to an end. She had enjoyed having Derrick's strong arm draped around the back of her seat, his hand occasionally dropping down to caress her shoulder. It had made her feel cared for . . . almost protected.

After the movie let out, the two of them walked slowly down the sidewalk. Jeni was happy; they laughed and joked as they walked back to Jeni's apartment. He had a way of saying the most outrageous things while keeping a straight face, and Jeni's face had begun to ache from laughing so hard. With another roll of laughter, she panted out, "Oh, Derrick, you should go on tour. You are hilarious!" She had to slow down even further to catch her breath as they neared her apartment door. "I have had such a good time, I hate for the evening to come to a close." She looked up into his eyes, smiled and was secretly glad Rosalyn was visiting her folks that weekend. She hoped that she and Derrick could put some music on and dance. Or better yet, just talk and get to know each other better.

Derrick put an arm around her waist as she turned the key in the lock. She pushed the door open and he pulled her close to himself. "It doesn't have to end yet," he half pleaded as his eyes penetrated hers.

Jeni's heart skipped a beat as she allowed him to gently nudge her inside and enfold her again in his arms. With a shove of his foot, Derrick pushed the door shut just before his searching, overheated lips touched hers. Her lips responded as he pressed her body against his own. Jeni melted in his arms, wishing this moment could last forever. She was not prepared when Derrick's hand slipped to the buttons on her blouse.

"Oh no, Derrick, no!" she implored. "I've decided not to do this anymore." She tried to shove him away, but her thin arms were no match for his bulk and muscle. Within herself, Jeni could feel something crumple. She whimpered again, "no," but she could offer no more resistance. Derrick took the lack of fight as permission, and he clumsily did what he wanted to with her body. When it was over, she sobbed, "Why did you? I told you no!"

Derrick's eyebrows pulled downward like thunderclouds and Jeni shivered. "You said no, but you really meant yes, and you know it," Derrick said with implacable ice in his voice.

Jeni's sudden anger spurted up and over the fear. "I meant just what I said," she screamed. "NO! NO! NO!"

Derrick shrugged his shoulders into his shirt, yanked his coat on and started for the door. Stung by the accusation, Derrick turned for one last parting shot. "Everyone knows you're easy, Jen. Don't try making out like you didn't want what you got." The door slammed behind him.

The pain howled in Jeni's ears and the darkness threatened to overwhelm her. Used. Used and thrown out, like a grubby tissue. Used. Where was the love? Where was the caring? Shattered illusions, like glittering shards of a mirror, cut deeply into her soul.

With gut-wrenching sobs, Jeni grabbed up her robe and pulled it around herself. Stumbling, she got up and bolted the apartment door behind Derrick, then slumped onto the couch beside the phone. Morning. She could make it to the morning. Just stay right there and wait for the light to come. *Oh please, let me make it through until the morning*, she thought to herself, *until I can reach Carol by phone at her office.*

CHAPTER 5

Damaged Goods

As Carol was unlocking her office door the next morning, she heard the phone begin to ring. Opening the door, she strode quickly across the office. Her left hand dumped her purse on the desk as her right hand picked up the handset. "Hello. Carol Gambavini." She moved around the side of the desk and pulled out her chair. "Hello?" Sitting down, she reached with her other hand and pulled a pen out of her purse. "Hello," Carol said into the phone, "is anyone there?" She waited a moment more, then with a sigh began to pull the handset away from her ear as she prepared to hang up. A thread of sound made her pause midmotion.

"Carol," the voice barely whispered, "help me."

Carol's forehead creased. The voice was too low for her to know which of her clients this could be. "Who is this?" she asked, patiently waiting for an answer.

"It's me, Jeni." Just making contact with her psychologist gave her encouragement. Carol was there. Carol cared. "I really need to see you." Her voice grew a bit stronger.

"What's the problem, Jeni?"

"I can't . . . I can't talk about it over the phone."

"Okay, Jeni. Let me see what I can swing here," Carol replied as she consulted her appointment book. "Can you make it until noon?"

"I think so," her client drawled with some uncertainty.

"Right. Now, Jeni, tell me exactly what you are going to do between now and then."

Carol could hear the puzzlement in her client's voice. "Why?"

Carol made sure the reassuring smile was in her own voice. "Because if you have already made plans about what you are going to do, then you aren't nearly as likely to do something else that you'll regret. It's a way to help you make it until I can see you."

"Oh. Oh, okay. I can see that." There was a pause on the line as Jeni thought it through. Carol could hear the catch in Jeni's voice. The therapist knew how hard it was for her client to try and focus on the everyday things right now, but also knew it would help her get through this latest crisis, whatever had sparked it off.

"Maybe you could get some breakfast?"

"I don't feel much like eating."

"Mmmm. I understand that, Jeni. But you do need to eat something. Not eating can make any depression worse, and you need your strength to face whatever has happened. How about some toast. Will you promise me to eat some toast?"

A sound halfway between a laugh and a sob came to Carol's ear. "Yeah, okay boss. I promise to eat some toast. And then I'll clean the apartment, and then it will be time to come see you."

"Good, Jeni. Sounds like a plan!" Carol put as much support and sturdiness in her voice as she could. "I'll see you then," Carol said as she entered Jeni's name into her appointment book. Once

Jeni had disconnected, she gently laid the handset back into its cradle.

*   *   *

Jeni was leaning wearily against the hallway wall, watching the office door. It seemed it would never open. She had gotten here early, and although she knew she should have checked in with the receptionist, she had ducked through one of the side corridors. She could not, she just could not face anyone right now and the waiting room always had people in it.

Carol's office door eventually did open and the last client for the morning left. Jeni stood frozen in place, trying to muster up the emotional and physical strength to go into the office. While she hesitated, Carol walked out of the doorway and headed for the waiting area to see if Jeni might be there. Jeni stepped away from the wall, her shoulders hunched inward. Carol stopped and gave her client a small smile before holding out her hand and softly beckoning, "Come on in, Jeni."

Jeni cringed across the room and perched on the edge of her usual chair. She sat still then, head bowed and trembling in starts and fits. Silence hung in the air for a moment before she could gather enough of herself to whisper, "I hate myself . . . I . . . I am a terrible person." Although her words were soft and broken, their message came through loud and clear.

"Why? What has convinced you that you are a terrible person, Jeni?"

"Be . . . because if . . ." her shoulders began shaking as the tears flowed down her face. "Because if I were any good, I would have made him stop."

Carol's eye's sharpened. This sounded all too familiar to her experienced ears. Keeping her voice both purposeful and gentle, Carol prodded Jeni slightly. "Mmm. Did you try?"

Jeni dashed a hand across her eyes. "Not hard enough,"

she gulped out in a hoarse whisper. The sobs grew deeper. "Maybe I deserved it."

"Mmm. Somehow, I doubt that Jeni," Carol encouraged. "What happened?"

"I . . . I was . . . I . . . . don't know" Jeni had no words for what had happened. Bad sex? A bad date? "He . . . my date, he wanted to . . . to go to bed, but I didn't. I told him . . . ." Jeni stammered softly.

Carol reached out a hand and placed it on the arm of Jeni's chair. "Jeni, were you raped?"

Jeni shuddered and looked up. "R-raped?"

Carol nodded. "Yes. Did a man force you to have sex when you didn't want to?"

Jeni broke down completely, sobbing convulsively so hard that she could not speak. Carol handed her a box of tissues and waited for the storm to calm a bit. "Oh Carol! Rosalyn told me I didn't have to anymore . . . that I didn't have to unless I wanted to. She said, just tell him 'no'." Jeni gulped for air. "I said 'no'. I said 'no' a lot. But he did it anyway," Jeni blew her nose and sniffled. "I feel so dirty . . . no good." She gazed at the used tissue in her hand and shuddered.

"Jeni. Listen to me. You are *not* dirty. You *are* a good person." Carol tapped the chair arm to make sure she had Jeni's attention. "Bad things **do** sometimes happen to good people. You did nothing at all to deserve this." Jeni was listening, but shook her head in negation. "Jeni, I have to ask you; do you want to report this to the police?"

Jeni flung up her head, her eyes wide in panic. "**No!** No, please Carol, no. Don't make me! Please don't be mad at me, but I can't."

Carol sat further back in her chair, her hands splayed in the air in front of her, gesturing to her client that no one would force her. "That's okay, Jeni. You don't have to if you don't want to. But I had to ask." Jeni stared at her, wide—eyed and trembling. "Jeni, it's okay. Do you understand?" With a convulsive shudder, Jeni nodded.

Carol pursed her lips a bit. "Jeni, I want to ask you something. It might be very hard. May I ask you?"

Jeni looked at Carol. She trusted Carol. Carol only asked the hard questions to try and help her, and she was grateful for that. Her face mirrored her feelings; looking like a lost and forlorn child, Jeni nodded again.

"This wasn't the first time that something like this has happened to you, is it."

Jeni recoiled. She knew! *How* could she know? She tried to clamp down on the memories flooding her, pushing her in front of them like a piece of driftwood. The wave built higher and more powerful, sweeping her resistance away. With a shriek, the tidal wave crested. "**Granddaddy! Granddaddy, NO!**" Jeni curled forward in on herself, twisting under the assault of the pain. "No . . . oh, no . . . ." she whimpered, rocking herself and hugging herself as tight as she could.

For awhile there was nothing more than the pain and the quiet murmur of Carol's voice, "I'm here, Jeni. I'm here for you."

Almost inaudibly, Jeni eventually whispered, "My granddaddy . . ." Louder she shrieked, "My granddaddy . . . I hate him . . . I **hate him**!" It was hard to imagine such fierce intensity coming out of this quiet, desperate soul. "Do you know what he did to me? He raped me, too, just like Derrick did last night!" Curling back in on herself, she seemed to sag in defeat. "Only Granddaddy did it many, many times."

"And each time, you felt used, didn't you."

Jeni's haunted eyes sought Carol's. "How did you know?"

Carol cocked her head and brought it down closer to Jeni's current eye level. She smiled sadly. "Most people who have been through this feel used. And the feeling comes from the awareness somewhere inside you that what that person did was as selfish as selfish gets."

"Selfish?" Jeni frowned in thought for a moment. "I . . . . I guess so."

"Jeni, when someone does whatever they want, no matter

how it hurts another person, then that is selfish. They are only thinking about what they want. Not about how it effects other people. They don't care that much about other people."

Brushing back a lock of blonde hair, Jeni struggled with this new concept, and tried to see if it fit her grandfather. "Sometimes he acted like he cared. But . . . well, I guess if he really had, he wouldn't have hurt me, would he?"

Carol shook her head with a sigh. "No. If he had cared more about you than about his own wants, then he wouldn't have hurt you." Carol paused for a moment, looking at her client as she considered. "You've had a poor self image for a long, long time haven't you?"

Jeni looked up and shook her head. She did not understand, but she answered. "Uh, yes, 'bout as long as I can remember."

"Did you know that pretty much everyone who has gone through what you have, has terrible self-esteem? It could be why you have such a horribly poor self-image, too."

Jeni straightened up with a rather startled expression, then slumped again. "I should have stopped them."

"How old were you when Granddaddy first touched you wrongly?"

Jeni gulped, but for the moment she could look at the memories without feeling overwhelmed. "Let's see, I was . . . in kindergarten. That would have made me five or six."

"Was he much larger than you?" Carol asked.

"Oh yes," Jeni hastily responded. "He was as big as my dad."

Carol pressed her point. "How could a little five or six year-old girl defend herself against a grown man?"

Silence . . .

"I don't know," Jeni mumbled. "When I tried to, he threatened me. He even hit me really hard one time. Another time, he slammed me onto the bed. I was so scared of him. He called it a game. I hated that game so much that I pretended in my head that I wasn't even there. It got so that I didn't remember what happened after he started hurting me."

"A young child like you were then is pretty defenseless against a grown up. And amnesia under those circumstances is not unusual. One could say that you were damaged by him, and you were. He didn't just damage your body when he hurt you physically, but he damaged your trust in others, and especially he damaged your ability to trust in yourself . . . . You were absolutely not at fault, Jen," Carol softly stated. She gave Jeni a few moments to absorb what she had said and concluded with, "So many people who have gone through rapes and molestation feel like damaged goods, and even use those exact words so often, that the therapists call it the 'Damaged Goods Syndrome'. You aren't alone in how you feel, Jeni."

Jeni listened, and thought about what Carol had said. After a moment she looked up. "Okay, so as a kid, I couldn't help myself, but I'm an adult now. I did not stop Derrick last night." Jeni inflicted more condemnation onto herself. "What's the matter with me? I didn't want to. Why did I let him do that?"

"Freezing like you did," her therapist explained, "is typical behavior for a person that was repeatedly molested in childhood, as you were."

"Why is that?" Jeni asked, truly trying to understand.

"Did your granddaddy threaten you about making any noise or about fighting him or about telling your folks?"

"Oh yes. Hmmmm," Jeni tried to absorb the counsel of this wise woman. "How can I avoid another fiasco like the one with Derrick?"

Carol nodded at her in approval. "Exactly the right question; you need to be able to trust yourself to protect yourself as much as possible. You're a smart young lady. Be careful not to put yourself at risk. Think ahead. Socialize in groups. Don't provide an opportunity for anyone to take advantage of you."

Carol nodded again and gave Jeni a smile. "Ready to take on the world again until next Tuesday?"

Jeni smiled weakly in return. "Yeah, I guess so."

Carol smiled at her warmly. "You know how to get a hold

of me before then if you need to." They both stood and Carol opened the door for her client.

"Thanks, Carol. Thank you so much for being there." Jeni turned, pulled her shoulders a little straighter, and walked down the hallway.

CHAPTER 6

A Cry for Help

Help!

Jeni had tried. She really had. But the turmoil of the after math of the rape and the resurfacing of the molestations were too much. Jeni could not go anywhere, even classes, without flinching every time a man looked in her direction. It was too much for her to handle. She decided not to register for the next semester.

* * *

Jeni grimaced and unconsciously shook her head as she held the phone's handset to her ear. "Mom, I can't go on like this. Since I dropped out of college, there's nothing left for me."

"Oh, sure there is," Cindy tried to reassure her daughter.

"Like what?" Jeni retorted. "I don't fit in with my druggie friends anymore and I can't hack the college scene. What am I supposed to do with myself?"

"What about your crafts? You've enjoyed them and you're talented in what you do," Cindy suggested.

"Oh come on, Mom. There should be more to life than crafts." Jeni twisted the phone cord around her wrist. "I had a doctor's appointment the other day. There still isn't much that can be done." Jeni hunched in on herself. "Let's face it, Mom. With my health, I can't foresee any kind of career. My life is just plain hopeless."

"Jeni dear, there are still many interesting things you can do. You just have to look for them. Why don't you get on your computer and search the web for something meaningful that you can do?"

Jeni sighed. "I'm not up to that, Mom."

"You love to read," Cindy said persuasively, trying desperately to help her child. "I'll check some good books out of the library for you to read. Tell me what you'd like."

Jeni threw out a hand in negation although her mother would not see it. "I don't even want to read. Life isn't worth living. It's too much of a struggle."

Cindy's concern echoed clearly in her voice. "At least let me come get you and take you out for awhile, maybe to the mall. Or you could come back home for a few days."

Jeni clenched her teeth in irritation. "No, Mom. Just leave me be!" Just as suddenly as the irritation had flared, she as quickly seemed to wilt. Everything was just simply too much effort. "I'm so tired . . . I gotta go," Jeni said before hanging up the phone.

*   *   *

Cindy was well and truly alarmed. She remembered the times Jeni had slashed her arms and had even used the oven to poison herself with natural gas. Cindy did not know what was wrong that caused Jeni such terrible pain that she would do these things; she felt helpless. What could she do for her daughter? With great distress, Cindy visualized the many crises followed by hospitalizations.

Oh God! Cindy cried silently in desperation for her daughter's safety. *You know I have tried to be a good mother. I don't know what to do now. Please Lord, protect Jeni from herself and lead her to You. Guide me Father God, in whatever I can do. In Jesus' Name I pray. Amen.* She rested her head in her hands on the kitchen table.

A moment later, Cindy lifted her head. She had quite suddenly and clearly had the thought of the name of a woman she knew. A Christian friend who lived outside of a nearby town. A tiny seed of hope began. *Dee does seem very knowledgeable. She has helped others in their Christian walk. I've already told her about Jeni's poor health and emotional problems*, Cindy thought. Pushing up from the table, Cindy began looking for the book she had gotten from Dee. She knew that she had written her phone number down in the inside cover.

Finding the book, Cindy hesitated for only a moment before dialing. Taking a deep breath, she waited as the phone rang. When Dee answered, it felt as if a weight had shifted slightly off of Cindy's shoulders. She explained to Dee about how down Jeni was and about her own concern for her. "I don't think she'll get any better until she accepts Jesus into her life. Will you *please* visit her, Dee?" Cindy pleaded.

"I'll pray about it," Dee answered. "I don't believe I can help her unless God is leading me." She reached out to sooth and encourage Cindy. "Nothing will work until He is ready, Cindy. He'll know when it's the right time . . . when it is the time that Jeni is ready to listen."

*   *   *

Dee did pray, for Cindy, Jeni and for guidance. But she never felt that God was telling her, 'now' was the time to talk to Jeni herself. It remained that way for a couple of months. One morning, however, Dee awoke with Jeni on her mind. Throughout the morning, thoughts of the troubled young woman would rise up in her consciousness, unbidden. Dee prayed again, and felt the definite answer. It was time. Dee called Jeni's mother. "I believe this is the day I should meet Jeni. Will you go with me?"

"I sure will!" Cindy was excited. "Do you want directions so you can meet me there?"

"No, Cindy, I'll pick you up on the way."

"I will be ready. Just honk your horn and I'll be right out," Cindy stated, almost beside herself with glee. Within thirty minutes she heard three short horn blasts. She scooped up her purse then sprinted from her home, swooping down the steps and into Dee's car like a sparrow. After greeting each other, the women's conversation turned to Jeni.

Cindy shook her head, trying to piece the mosaic together and failing. "I don't know what happened to my daughter. She was such a beautiful, happy, willing little girl." Dee listened intently as Cindy continued, obviously distraught. "I read her Bible stories. She and I sang songs about Jesus together. She knew Jesus loves her, just like her dad and I do. I took her to Sunday School and church regularly as she grew up. We were good to her." Cindy stopped and looked at her hands lying in her lap.

"It was almost as if she changed overnight." Her hands gripped each other. "Why has she been so rebellious?"

Not waiting for an answer, Cindy shook her head and continued. "My caring and sensitive little girl became irritable and angry. She started instigating trouble with my other children and the neighborhood kids. At times the kids were vehement about her misbehavior and Jeni was just as adamant about her innocence. At first, I didn't know who to believe, but soon I had to admit that Jeni sometimes seemed to start trouble just because she could." Cindy drew in a deep breath. She had not felt free with anyone else to talk so openly about the problems she had faced with her daughter. In a real way it was a relief, even if a very sad one.

Her chin lifted slightly as she went on. "As she grew into her teens the problems continued and she became obviously depressed. She was a tremendously troubled teenager. We didn't know what to do. Then, after a checkup the doctor recommended a full medical work up. Afterwards, the doctors said she had lupus. They also said that her health was a part of her problems."

Cindy sighed. "She's been under mental health care for fourteen years." She gulped back a sob. "There have been so many times, dozens of times, where Jeni has had to be put in the hospital because she tried to hurt herself. I hate remembering it all; she's cut herself and taken drug overdoses, and she's tried to kill herself by sticking her head in an unlit gas oven." Cindy turned for a moment and stared blindly out the car window. After a time, she was able to continue. "I've tried to be there for her. I always have. But she won't listen to me anymore and I feel like I've failed my child."

Dee had been both listening intently and praying silently while her friend had opened her heart to her. Compassion for her friend's heartache was strong and deep; Dee remembered when one of her own children had rebelled as a teenager, and how hard that had been on her and her husband. Now Dee spoke gently. "There's no way to know at this time what the future holds for Jeni. One encouraging scripture says 'Train a child in the way he should go, and when he is old, he will not turn from it'. That's in Proverbs 22:6."

"That *is* encouraging, Dee." Cindy breathed deeply and smiled a little. "I'll continue to love her and pray for her, just like I always have."

"Is she a Christian?" Dee asked.

"I do not think so," was Cindy's sad response.

"Does she go to church?" Dee probed, attempting to gain enough background information in order to minister to Jeni's needs.

"Not anymore," Cindy reluctantly answered. She went on to explain, "There was a woman who prayed with her and took her to church a few times. Then this lady called Jeni and said she wouldn't be seeing her anymore and that Jeni was not to call her either. I guess this lady had tried all she could think of to help my daughter. Jeni became very angry. She threw the Bible across the room and cursed God something fierce." Cindy pulled out a tissue and caught her tears. "It broke my heart! How could Jeni act like that? I couldn't believe my ears." Cindy concluded.

As they neared the street that Jeni lived on, Cindy worked hard to regain her composure. She did not want to do anything that might endanger Jeni taking whatever help that Dee might offer her.

Jeni's apartment was on the top floor of a private home with an outside entrance. The two women climbed the open wooden staircase and knocked on the door. Dee saw a surly and somewhat hostile twenty-three year-old woman, who grudgingly opened the door and motioned for her mother and Dee to come inside. After just a few moments of small talk, Jeni told them, "You gotta go now. I have an appointment at mental health."

"I can drive you there if you'd like," Dee offered. Jeni blinked in surprise but then seemed to realize the offer was genuinely based in pure helpfulness. Dee dropped Jeni off at the mental health clinic, then she and Cindy traveled the highway that led home.

*   *   *

Jeni plopped down in her usual chair in Carol's office. "Does it ever seem to you that my problems just don't get better. I mean, why am I still having the nightmares and blank outs? Why do I still feel depressed most of the time? Why are these voices in my head still tormenting me? Why aren't I getting any better?"

Carol carefully assessed her client. "You do get better Jeni. But then, after a while you seem to have setbacks." Carol gazed at the young woman. "Are you certain that you really do, deep down, want to get better?"

Startled, Jeni sat up straight and stared at her therapist. "Yes! Yes I want to get better! Why would you ask that?"

Carol shrugged. "Because a lot of people don't *really* want to get better."

Jeni's head went back, her chin tucked into her neck. "That's just plain weird. And anyway, I *do* want to get better."

Carol smiled slightly. "Then I would have to say that there is something else, something we don't yet know about, that is standing in your way. Something deep inside yourself that is sabotaging your efforts."

Jeni sat back and pondered awhile on this new thought. Eventually, she looked back up. "Well, then, how do we find it?"

Carol nodded her approval. "We keep working to clean up the things we do know about. We pull on them some and see if we can find the threads that lead to that deeper thing."

Jeni gave a sigh. "Okay. So, where were we . . . ."

*   *   *

It was six months later. Jeni had been working to try and find that deep—rooted something that kept her from getting better, but neither she nor Carol had found it yet. The darkness was gathering again, and the pain screeched at the back of Jeni's skull as if trying to dig its way out of her brain pan. She knew she was in trouble. She could feel the edges of her resolve giving away under the onslaught. Voices . . . from her past, from inside . . . taunting her, reviling her, pinching at her soul with vise-like fingers of despair.

Desperate, Jeni tried focusing her thoughts somewhere else. Almost blindly, she reached for a book from her shelf. When she looked down, she found she had picked up the book of Dee's that her mother had given to her. Feeling like she was clutching at straws, Jeni curled into the overstuffed chair and began to try and read. Daylight had to come sometime. This might just help her make it until then.

*   *   *

Dee's telephone rang at five-thirty in the morning. Trying to blink the sleep from her eyes, Dee stumbled out of bed and to the phone. "Hello."

"I am afraid I am going to kill myself," cried the frightened voice. "I found your phone number in the book that Mom gave me . . ."

"Who are you?" Dee interrupted, trying to sharpen her focus.

"Jeni! You came to my apartment with my mom. Don't you remember?"

"Oh yes, now I remember," Dee assured her.

Jeni continued, "All night I've heard voices in my head. 'Turn on the gas, it won't take long. Go ahead! Life is the pits. It's not worth the struggle.' Then I remembered that Mom had jotted down your phone number in this book she had given me. I kept hearing her voice saying, 'I think Dee can help you.' I've tried to wait 'til daybreak, but I was afraid I wouldn't make it."

Knowing that Jeni's health was poor and remembering how moving to the country had helped improve the health of her asthmatic son, Dee thought a visit for Jeni to her country home might be helpful. She was also aware that this young woman needed love and prayer support. Dee offered, "Would you like to come to my house for a few days? I live in the country."

"I, uh, I guess so," Jeni stammered.

"It'll take me about an hour to get to you. Can you hang in there that long?"

"I'll try," Jeni said weakly and hung up the phone.

"Lord, please help her," Dee prayed. She continued to pray while she dressed and took care of what needed to be done for her family in her absence. Then she left for the city, to find and bring this disturbed young woman to her home.

CHAPTER 7

Depression or Possession

Jeni waited, fidgeting. She had packed a few clothes and was as ready as she would be for this unexpected visit. She was worried and depressed. What if Dee decided she did not like her? What really was she expecting Dee to do for her that no one else had? And would Dee even want to help? When she heard the car drive up and park in the street below, she sat frozen for a moment. She was afraid to hope. Afraid of being rejected, as she had been rejected so many times before. Even as she sat still, however, she could feel the swirling of the encroaching darkness in the back of her mind. She had to take this chance.

Dee seemed genuinely welcoming, but Jeni knew that many

people were . . . at first. Afraid, she was withdrawn and depressed as she put her luggage in the back of Dee's car and then sat herself in the front seat. The twenty-five mile drive into the country from Jeni's place was not only an attractive one, but also a peaceful one. As they turned off the blacktop onto a dirt road, they passed an old apple orchard and a huge old barn. Soon, the one hundred and thirty-year old farmhouse came into view. Dee turned into the driveway just before the dirt road led into the woods. The nearest house to Dee's was a mile away.

Once inside, Jeni followed Dee to a bedroom that she could use as her own while visiting. "Make yourself at home," Dee said. Jeni was still afraid, and she could not force herself to speak. Instead, she nodded her head. Dee beckoned to her, and Jeni followed. She found herself in a pleasant room, the colors a calm and quiet blend of greens. It seemed to mirror the woods outside the house. Across one wall there was a huge built-in bookcase, filled with all sorts of books.

Suddenly wary, she could feel Dee's eyes on her. Turning, she found the older woman's compassionate, warm dark eyes looking at her. "I have some work I need to do, then we'll spend time together later today. Help yourself to any of the books on the bookshelf if you'd like to do some reading, or you can take a walk down the road, if you'd like," Dee suggested.

Jeni thought for a moment. "Then I'll take a walk since it's okay." She needed some neutral space where she could regain her sense of balance. Dee's miniature schnauzer, Butch, sniffed at Jeni's shoes and the young woman bent down to pat his head. As Jeni went out the door, Butch followed her. "Do you want to come?" Butch gazed up at her and wagged his stub of a tail. She smiled and motioned to him; the two went down the steps and into the woods in total accord.

The peace within the shelter of the huge trees was just what Jeni's battered soul had needed. She walked slowly, smiling at Butch's gentlemanly attempts to show her all the important sites, such as the openings to the ground hog dens. Here there were no fingers pointing in accusation; there was only a friendly dog frisking about and enjoying her company. After a time, Jeni felt they had gone far enough. Calling Butch, she turned their steps back towards the house. Jeni felt less anxious than she had in a long time. With the fears momentarily at bay, she went into her room to unpack, Butch right behind her.

After supper was eaten and the dishes were done, Jeni and Dee sat on the front porch. Jeni looked out past the dirt road and watched the water flow and sparkle in the brook on the other side. Jeni heard Dee's indrawn breath and turned to face her, knowing that it was time to talk. "Tell me, Jeni, why do you think you get so depressed?" Dee inquired.

Jeni hedged. She did not know Dee very well at all. "Partly because of my poor health," she responded. "I have lupus pretty bad and it keeps me sick a lot."

"You said 'partly'; is there something else?"

"I, uh . . . . It's really hard to talk about. I guess there are several reasons." Jeni was trying hard to be open; she had learned that much from Carol. No one can help if they do not know the truth. Even still, it was hard to trust this stranger. Her feet forced the porch swing she was sitting in to move more vigorously. "I was raped many times. I have awful nightmares about that. It really bothers me a lot."

"How long ago was that?" Dee pressed.

Jeni took in a deep breath, then slowly let it out. "A while back, when I was in college." She hesitated a fraction, then steeled herself to continue. "But there were others before college."

"Did you have any depression before college?" Dee persisted.

Jeni swallowed hard, caught her breath, then softly answered, "Actually, I did for many years." Jeni forced herself to go on. "I was molested as a kid. My therapist says depression is not uncommon for a young incest victim. The doctor told me that what my granddaddy did to me so often when I was little may have even played a big part in my poor health."

Jeni was trembling. The effort to reveal so much was hard. To trust that Dee would not use it to hurt her later was even harder. Dee noticed the strain Jeni was under, so she gave her a few moments to relax with small talk. Slowly, after Jeni was calm again, Dee brought the conversation back to the problem at hand. "How long have you been troubled with suicidal thoughts?"

"Oh, off and on since high school, maybe even before that." To Jeni, it seemed that she had always longed for some kind of ultimate escape. A thought creased her forehead. Timidly, Jeni said, "I'd like to ask you a question, okay?"

"Go ahead," Dee encouraged her guest.

The fears of rejection crowed close."Promise you won't be mad at me . . . or hate me." Jeni implored.

"I won't be mad. Ask away, dear," Dee stated.

"Is there anyway I can kill myself without going to hell? I don't want to go to hell." Jeni's tears freely cascaded down her cheeks.

Dee's heart was broken and the mother in her reached over to enfold this troubled young lady in her arms. "Oh, honey, God loves you. He'll help you through this without suicide, if you'll let Him."

The icy grip of the fear relented in the face of the obvious care and concern Dee felt. With a sigh, Jeni let herself sink into the warmth. She rested her head on Dee's shoulder, feeling comforted and cared about. They swung lightly for several minutes.

                              *   *   *

The peepers were sounding off in the dark fields around them and the temperature began to drop a bit. When they felt the chill, the two women rose and went into the house. Dee sat at the kitchen table, with Jeni following her example. "Let's read from the Bible and have prayers before retiring for the evening," Dee said as she reached for the Bible. Dee heard a little moan escape from her guest's lips. She looked up from the Bible to see Jeni's eyes rolled back and her head jerking at weird angles. Jeni's hands went up in front of her face as if she were trying to defend herself.

"No, no, no!" Jeni cried hysterically.

Dee's eyes widened in astonishment. She set the Bible down, but Jeni did not calm down, so she pushed it further back across the table and away from Jeni. Dee was also silently praying for

God's help and guidance. Jeni suddenly turned on her. With hate-filled eyes and an intense, angry voice, Jeni bellowed, "Don't you **ever** do that again. I will **not** listen to that book or pray with you!"

"Then there is no way that I can help you," Dee said. "Without God I can do nothing." Jeni sat there stone-like. It was as if she had not heard. After a few minutes of silence, Dee continued. "I meant it. Without scripture and prayer, I **cannot** help you. You think about it. You can let me know in the morning what you decide."

"I'm getting ready for bed," Jeni stood and said to Dee. After a brief pause, she continued in a more normal voice, "Will you come in, in a little while and tell me good night?"

"Sure thing," Dee replied.

After a short time, Dee tapped on the bedroom door. Jeni called, "Come in," then patted the edge of the bed for Dee to sit down. "Will you sit with me until I fall asleep? I have such horrible nightmares. I'm embarrassed to say that I still sleep with the light on."

It was not long before Jeni's deep breathing indicated to Dee that she had fallen asleep; Dee nodded absently to herself and rose to go. There was no way for Dee to realize she was about to encounter the strangest and most difficult night she would ever remember.

It began softly at first. Dee already had her hand on the door knob to leave when she heard the first faint murmur. "No, no, no," Jeni began to moan quietly in her sleep. Dee hesitated, then returned to the bedside chair to try and sooth Jeni in her sleep. Within a few minutes, Jeni began to thrash from side to side. She kicked her legs and again cried out, "**No! Stop!**" Her head was thrown violently from one side of the pillow to the other. In disbelief, Dee watched as Jeni's hands clutched her own throat in a vise-like grip, so tightly that her face turned red. Her bulging eyes were now open as she glared sightlessly at unseen foes.

"In the name of Jesus, release her," Dee firmly commanded. Jeni's arms dropped and her demeanor soon returned to that of normal sleep. Dee soon found out that these periods of quiet sleep were short, however. The manifestations would always soon begin again. They only stopped when Dee quoted scripture, prayed or rebuked them.

*   *   *

Jeni woke the next morning to find Dee at her side. She smiled up at the older woman, but Dee seemed troubled and more distant than Jeni remembered her from the night before. "I'll let you get dressed, now." Dee rose and left the room.

After dressing, Jeni went looking for her host. She found Dee doing some paper work on the kitchen table, and warily sidled up and sat in one of the other chairs. "Is something wrong?"

Dee looked up. "No, Jeni. But it has to be up to you whether or not I can help you. Have you made your decision?"

Icicles of raw fear ran down on either side of Jeni's spinal column. Made her decision? About what? "Please don't give up on me. I really want help. Don't listen if something else comes out of my mouth. Please . . . **please!**"

"Why shouldn't I believe what you say?" Dee questioned.

"You're going to think I am crazy." Jeni flatly stated. "I get amnesia sometimes. The psych doc says it might be from all the sexual abuse in my childhood. Sometimes it's very short, like a few minutes or hours. Occasionally it lasts a few days." Jeni tried to work some saliva into her mouth so she could continue. "When I know what's going on again, I find people are mad at me for what I've said or done. Things I don't remember doing. Things, sometimes, that . . . well . . . that's hard for me to believe that I have done. I've just can't hardly believe that I would *ever* do some of the things they've accused me of." She looked down at the table, her shoulders hunched inward. "I've had this problem for as long as I can remember."

Having been an active registered nurse until her own health gave out, Dee was aware of disassociative mental problems. She knew that repeated, traumatic incestual experiences when the person had been a child could indeed result in such a fracture in the person's pysche. Jeni's periods of amnesia could be related to

this. However, Dee thought that her reactions to the Bible coupled
with the behavior during the nightmares appeared to be demonic.

Jeni interrupted Dee's thoughts. "There have been others who
have tried to help me. They've taken me to church and prayed
with me. The next thing I knew, they were mad at me and I didn't
know why."

"I'll make a contract with you. I will do whatever I can to help
you, Jeni, if you make a contract with me in return. That you'll be
one hundred percent honest in all you say and do with me."

"I promise," Jeni offered with fragile relief.

"I'll trust God to help me have discernment as to your situation
at all times," Dee also promised with a firm nod of her head.

"Then you'll still try to help me?" Jeni asked, hopeful as her
eyes brightened.

The former nurse gently took and held Jeni's hand sandwiched
between her own. "Jeni," she began softly, "I believe some demons
are abiding in you. Before we go any further, I need time to study
all that the Bible tells us about this kind of problem."

Jeni looked at her with puzzlement, but anything that might
help her was welcome. She nodded. "Okay."

*   *   *

Jeni was able to enjoy the country air and wide open spaces for
the remainder of that day and most of the next one before Dee
took her home. As they pulled in front of Jeni's apartment, Dee
told her, "I won't call you or bring you back to my place until I
have finished studying about your problems. So, you hang in there
until I get back to you, okay?"

"I will really try. Thanks Dee," Jeni said before climbing out
of her new friend's car.

As Dee drove home, she thought of the information in Dr.
Terri Clark's book, *More Than One*. Amnesia, blanking out and
extreme personality changes can be related to either serious mental
health problems, demon possession or both.

At home, Dee pulled the book off the shelf and reviewed the

chapter on possession versus pretending. One of the things that caught her attention was Dr. Clark's assertion that even though laboratory evidence cannot prove or disprove the existence of demons and demon possession, there is still a great deal of empirical evidence that demon possession does exist and is still occurring right now in the modern world.

Other insights on the manifestations of demons supported the discernment God was giving Dee. The hatred and bitterness that came from Jeni in response to the Bible was definitely pertinent. Dee thought about the passage in Ephesians 6:10-18 and was glad she had on the armor of God that it spoke of. She also thanked God for the authority and power He promised in Luke 10: 17—19 to those who truly serve Him.

CHAPTER 8

Deliverance Begun

Jeni's situation reminded Dee of Myrtle, a friend in a neighboring town who had been delivered of demons several years earlier. Myrtle was a descendant of a witch doctor and even had psychic powers herself. Dee remembered the scripture of Exodus 34: 7, and what it had to say about ancestral sorcery. Myrtle believed that Jesus is the Messiah, the Savior, but when she had tried to talk about Him, she would curse. Myrtle lived for years with overwhelming depression. Suicidal thoughts tortured her daily. Dee was one of the team that ministered to Myrtle, before and after she was delivered of evil spirits. Afterwards, Myrtle had been free to praise her Lord and to live without interference.

The pastor who had led that deliverance team stressed to them that it was vital to be a Bible-reading and praying Christian that is obedient to the Lord. He also emphasized the team should fast at least one meal before undertaking such a ministry. There were other instructions regarding this type of ministry as well. He told them to always cast out demons on God's territory . . . a church or a territory where Christ is acknowledged Lord, to not allow children or unsaved persons to be present, and he stressed that the candidate should have a desire to be delivered.

Unfortunately, that pastor had moved to a different state. In the present situation, Dee would be undertaking the responsibility for Jeni's deliverance. She took this responsibility very seriously and immediately began to search the scriptures to find Bible references on the situation. Her topical Bible and Bible encyclopedia were also helpful. In addition, Dee poured over several other books, including those written by missionaries, on the topic of deliverance.

As she was putting down one of the books by a missionary, Dee was reminded of a husband and wife team of pastors that she knew. They had been missionaries themselves for several years, most often in the Caribbean. She reached for her address book and found their number.

"Hi, Robin?" she asked when a female voice came on the line. "This is Dee. I'd like to talk to you and Garth about demon possession if I could."

"Dee! It's good to hear from you! Certainly, you can talk to us. Let me put this on the speaker."

"Hello, Dee," came Garth's baritone. "What would you like to know?"

"Well, Garth, let me describe some of what I have been seeing, and hear your own reaction." Dee recounted her observations of Jeni's behavior, the nightmares, and her reactions to the Bible and prayer.

"Oh, yes, Dee. We have seen all of those things," Robin said. "There was a great deal of demonic activity in the village where we were. What you are describing to us is very familiar. Especially the reactions to the Bible and to prayer."

"How would you approach the situation, then?" Dee asked.

"As with all things," Gareth said, "with a very firm grounding in prayer and a good, solid scriptural foundation. But we have found that when you are up against this kind of thing, you really need to bolster yourself with a lot of fasting. Remember to look up Mark 9: 29 in the King James, and also Matthew 6: 17 and 18. Casting out demons is not easy; it takes a lot of spiritual focus. Also, if they are persistent or very strong, the more believers who are there praying for the person's deliverance, the better chance there is that you will be able to force them out."

Robin spoke up. "Dee, we'll send this out as a prayer request to the other pastors we know. The more Christians you have fasting and praying for both Jeni and you, the better." Robin paused for a brief second. "Dee, you should also keep notes on all of this. I feel that they might be very beneficial should you or another Christian run into such a situation again."

Dee thanked them both. It was reassuring to hear what they had to tell her on the subject, since she knew that their Christian foundations ran deep and that they had had experience with delivering people from demons.

The days of study continued. As always, Dee maintained an active prayer life, adding the situation and the preparations to her prayer list. Even during the preparation stages, she felt guided to fast many meals as she prayed, researched and prepared.

*   *   *

Dee stood and stretched after many long hours in front of her computer. It had been a month since she had begun her intense preparation for ministry to Jeni's specific needs. Dee had readied herself for this coming confrontation with much fasting, prayer, and study. She had made every effort she could to prepare herself and now had the faith that God's Holy Spirit would guide her in what was to follow. As she closed the Bible and Bible encyclopedia and organized her papers, Dee told her husband, "I have finally finished my research on demon possession and how to deal with it."

At that precise moment the phone rang. "I've tried not to call," Jeni apologized, "but the voices in my head have become fierce. I'm afraid of what I might do."

A warm smile spread over Dee's face. The Lord's timing was simply amazing. "It's okay Jeni, I've just finished my study. Pack your things, enough for several days. I'm on my way to pick you up." Dee arrived at Jeni's apartment less than an hour later. Jeni was ready and waiting for her, her suitcase sitting next to her on the top step of her outside stairway. Dee smiled, chatted and did her best to alleviate some of Jeni's depression and anxiety on the journey back to her house.

The next morning after family members had left the house, Dee and Jeni sat on the couch in the family room. Dee's small schnauzer jumped onto the couch and snuggled down between them. Jeni smiled and gently stroked his ears before looking up at Dee. "I've always thought that if the animals still like me, I can't be all bad. They give me hope." Dee smiled and nodded. She, too, often felt that the animals were a good judge of character.

With a small mental shake, she set her thoughts firmly on the upcoming task. Remembering how Jeni had reacted when she had picked up the Bible on the previous visit, Dee decided to go through the deliverance session first, then perhaps this young woman would be more receptive to the Bible and prayer. Because of the terrible nightmares and persistent depression, Dee felt led to start with the spirits of nightmares and depression. If the depression were purely medical, no harm would be done. If Jeni's depression was not of a medical nature, this was certainly needed.

"Do you have nightmares often?" Dee inquired.

"Nearly every night. Sometimes it's my granddaddy and sometimes frightening fuzzy creatures. They are trying to rape me. I wake up breathless, totally exhausted and my neck hurts real bad." Jeni responded.

"The Bible tells us that demons sometimes enter people. They could be responsible for some of your nightmares and depression. Please understand that when I speak to evil spirits that I am not accusing or criticizing you."

Jeni did not say anything. Instead her face changed, just as it had on her previous visit when Dee had picked up the Bible. All of the muscles in Jeni's face completely relaxed, making her expression, or lack of one, look like a mask. Out of the deadly, trance-like stillness of this mask, the eyes glittered hard but unfocused.

Dee leaned on the verses of Matthew 10:8 and Mark 16: 17. Firmly, she spoke in rebuke. "Spirit of nightmares, I command you to leave Jeni's body in Jesus' name and by the power of His blood—Go!" In a flash, Jeni jumped up and ran out of the house and down the road. Dee followed to the door, watching and praying for Jeni's protection from the evil one. About ten minutes later, Jeni came back into the house, went to the family room at the back of the house and sat on the couch without saying a word.

The next time, Dee was prepared. Getting ready to rebuke the spirits again, she laid her hands one on each of Jeni's shoulders. "Demons of nightmares, I rebuke you in the name of Jesus and through the power of His blood. Leave Jeni, **now!**" Jeni's body strained to get up, but finding the effort blocked, almost immediately the energy went into a paroxysm of coughing. Then her head began banging against the back of the couch. Dee repeated the rebuke and after more coughing, her body relaxed.

Butch, the dog, had raised his head briefly but soon relaxed as if to take yet another nap. Very soon afterwards, Dee heard the front door open. "I'm home," Dee's husband Harv called as he came in the front door, a little earlier than usual.

"Hi, dear," Dee replied. Harv collected his newspaper and went to the living room at the front of the house where he reclined in his favorite chair to read. Dee breathed a silent prayer and then commanded, "In the name of Jesus and by the power of His blood, I command you, spirits of depression to leave this woman's body."

"I hate you . . . I hate you . . . **I hate you!**" were the angry words escaping from Jeni's lips. "I want to go home. Take me home, **right now!**"

Dee demanded once again, "I command you spirits of depression, leave her now in Jesus' name and by His power. Go **now!**"

Jeni gasped for air as the choking began. Dee commanded the spirits once more. It appeared as though Jeni either fainted or the demons were completely controlling her body as she slumped deep into the couch. "Harv," Dee called, "Harv, I need you!" He quickly joined the two women in the family room and Dee explained the situation.

Her husband then addressed the demons. "As the Bible tells us in Ephesians 5: 23, I am the God-given authority in this house. Your time is up! In the name of Jesus and by His blood, get out of here. Leave Jeni right now."

Jeni began to stir, slowly raising her upper torso and head. After a paroxysm of coughing, she quizzically looked at Dee.

"How are you?" Harv asked Jeni.

She shrugged her shoulders with the palms of her hands upwards as if to say she was not sure.

"Jeni," Dee said, "Harv and I have cast some demons of nightmares and depression out of you. Do you feel okay?" Jeni nodded her head affirmatively.

After the evening meal, Dee and Jeni sat down at the kitchen table. "Would you like to go home in the morning?" Dee asked.

Jeni's brow crinkled. "Oh, no. I . . . I thought I was going to stay several days?"

"I don't want to force any of this on you. If you stay, it must be because you want to." Dee said.

Bewilderment was clearly written on Jeni's face. "What do you mean, if I want to? I do want to with all my heart. I thought you knew that."

Dee rested her chin in her hand. "Earlier this afternoon, Jeni, you demanded that I take you home that instant."

"I said that?" Jeni was obviously distressed. "Oh Dee, please don't listen to anything I say when I'm blanked out. I do want your help . . . **please!**"

Dee silently contemplated the rising probability that Jeni's periods of amnesia and much of her behavior truly might be caused by one or more demons taking control of her body. She stood behind Jeni with her hands on the younger woman's shoulders. She pressed down lightly, preventing her from running away. Dee began to pray. There was some resistance, but Jeni did not leave the chair, only coughed during the prayer.

"Most gracious Heavenly Father, protect this child in these spiritual battles. Give her freedom to open her heart and mind to you, your Son and your Word. In Jesus' name, I pray. Amen." Dee sat down and reached across the table for the Bible. As she laid it between them, Jeni's reaction was much the same as on her last visit.

Jeni's hands blocked her face as she turned away, crying, "Stop! I won't look at it! *Get it away from me!*" Dee moved the Bible to the other side of the table. Dee watched Jeni for a moment, realizing that this war was not over yet. She nodded absently to herself. She should address reading the Bible and prayer during Jeni's next visit to her home.

*   *   *

Talking with Dee the following day, Jeni was shaken to find that there were several 'blank out' gaps in her memory of the day before. Some of what Dee told her was painfully reminiscent of other times when Christian people had tried to help her at first, only to walk away later in disgust. Jeni was nearly frozen in panic, afraid that Dee would reject her, too. She waited through the morning for the axe to fall, but by lunch had begun to notice that Dee was perfectly calm and matter-of-fact. She seemed concerned for Jeni, but not upset by her. Jeni's fears began to recede.

She stayed at Dee's for several more days. It was almost like a vacation for her; she was free to enjoy the beautiful outdoors, read and watch television. And even though she might seem withdrawn at times, inside a tiny coiled up bit of misery was noticing that she was being cared about and was grateful.

When finally the time came for Jeni to return to her home, during the drive Dee promised to bring her back to the country in two or three weeks. "But you call me, if you need me before I call you." Dee reassured her.

"Thanks again." Jeni's eyes misted. Words were not enough to express the mixture of hopeful feelings within her.

CHAPTER 9

Spiritual Warfare

Jeni got out of the car and breathed in the clean scents of the woods and fields. Although this was only her third visit to Dee's home, it felt well-known and reassuring. Jeni took her things to the room she stayed in, and happily settled in. That evening, Dee and Jeni spent the evening just companionably talking on the front porch. Jeni was still afraid to trust it, but she could feel a kind of contentment and peace here. It felt safe.

With surprise, Jeni found that she was readily able to tell Dee things that she had had to fight to tell even Carol. Through the evening, she found that her experiences and feelings seemed to just tumble out through their own accord. It began with telling

Dee about the lupus and how hard it was to feel 'normal' when she could not do everything the other kids her age were doing. How hard it had been to feel accepted, let alone included. How she felt that her poor health was like a wall separating her from the rest of the world.

From there, Jeni moved on to explaining to Dee how much higher that wall had seemed to become when she had been sent to see her first therapist. How difficult it was to cope with the label of mental illness and the fears of being crazy. She knew that there were things that were messed up inside her; how could she not know that? But, no matter how hard she tried, it seemed like she never got any better. She never found any peace inside.

Jeni was able to tell Dee about the constant anxiety. She told Dee more about the sexual abuse she had endured and how she felt about herself because of it. She explained how deep her fear of sleeping was, because it brought such horrible nightmares. She told Dee about the ways she had tried to escape all the pain, the confusion and the fear. How she had turned to drugs to try and dull the pain away, but the pain would not be dulled. It all poured out . . . that at least a part of her was convinced that the only way to be free was to be dead. She told Dee about the voices in her head that told her over and over that death was the doorway out. She told Dee about the times when she just could not take any more pain; the times when she attempted suicide. She told Dee about slashing her wrists and arms; she spoke about turning on her gas oven without allowing it to light and then sticking her head into it. Somehow, though, the end had never come.

Jeni looked at Dee. "Why would He punish me for suiciding? I want so much to put an end to this torment, but I don't want to go to hell," she said again to Dee. Dee cocked her head to the side a moment as she thought, then flipped open her Bible to Exodus 20: 13, reading what it had to say about suicide to Jeni. The young woman listened to Dee's scriptural responses, but her head then shook slightly. "I haven't been able to . . . you know . . . uh . . . pr . . . pr . . . pray for a long time or even look at the . . . uh . . . you know . . . that book."

"Do you mean the Bible?"

"Yes," Jeni confessed, "and I can't say . . . uh . . . His name either."

"Are you speaking of Jesus?" Dee asked.

"Yes," Jeni answered. "At least I haven't blanked out today. I could hear what you told me that the . . . uh, book said about murder . . . uh . . . killing oneself." Dee smiled at her in encouragement, and Jeni tentatively smiled back.

When the two of them finally entered the house to retire for the night, it was nearly daybreak. There were still some nightmares, although not as often or as intense as during Jeni's first visit.

*   *   *

Jeni's new freedom to talk about and listen to Dee's paraphrasing of God's words brought Dee a great deal of encouragement. The deliverance session she had planned for the next day, now only a few hours away, would begin with casting out anti-prayer spirits.

Dee prayed over Jeni and demanded the anti-prayer demons leave her. As before, Jeni had tried to rise, but Dee's firm hands on her shoulders kept her in her chair. As Dee continued to pray, Jeni coughed severely for a few minutes, and then became still and calm. Dee gathered herself for the next thrust. Firmly, she commanded the anti-Bible spirits to leave Jeni.

Dee immediately found herself in the center of a storm. Abruptly, the schnauzer yiped as if stung, jumped off the couch and ran to the other side of the room where he crouched in the corner, shaking. At the same moment, Jeni's hands gripped like vises on her own trachea, choking herself. Her body began to gag and retch as the airflow was cut off. When there was enough air in her lungs, the gagging would stop just long enough for a vitreous cry to emerge. "I hate you!" The gagging would immediately take over again as soon as the air in the lungs was used up. Suddenly, like a worn rag doll's head shaken with passionate force, Jeni's head flung violently in all directions. Her eyes bulged and her expression was wild. There was a frightening gurgling sound and her color had become ashen.

"**Harv!**" Dee screamed. "Harv, come quickly!"

The intensity of Dee's call brought her husband immediately. The two of them tried to still Jeni's flinging, swirling head. "Oh Lord, please protect her," Dee prayed. Harv rebuked the demons. Dee and Harv prayed as they held Jeni's head and shoulders tightly to protect her from these unbelievable gyrations.

Bit by bit, the thrashing of her head slowed and eventually stopped. The tension ebbed away from her muscles and her body slowly relaxed. While Dee continued to hold Jeni, Harv went to the next room to call their pastor. "Pastor Thomson, this is Harv. The young lady that Dee had asked you to pray for is here and the demonic spirits are too strong for us."

"Bring her to the church," Reverend Thomson directed. "I'll have some of the lay leaders here to help us."

"Thank you, Lord, for your caring servants," Dee breathed.

Jeni had to be pulled, pushed and cajoled to the car. It took both Dee and Harv to accomplish it, and once at the church, Jeni still attempted to avoid entering the building. Her facial expression, as before, had become trance-like, completely and totally non-responsive. Once Jeni was seated inside the church, Dee, Harv, two pastors and two lay leaders surrounded her. They prepared to prevent the vise-like grip on her throat and any efforts to run away. Being in the house of God helped, and having six Christians now praying also increased the available power of God against the demonic powers that were preventing Jeni from reading the Bible, God's Holy Word.

It would have been useless to try and orient Jeni to the coming procedure. She was blanked out and unaware. Dee went ahead and began. "In the name of Jesus and by the power of Jesus' blood, we command you anti-Bible spirits to leave this body. Come out of her, now!" The resistance, such as grabbing her throat or trying to run, was relatively mild. The added help of these devout Christians, the added protection of their arms and their additional prayers sped and facilitated the success of this session.

Rather suddenly, Jeni's mind resurfaced. "I feel sick to my stomach." Jeni said with a slight retching motion. She gagged a couple of times, then coughed. These were not light coughs but the deep, searing kind of cough found with pneumonia. Eventually, even these too faded away, leaving a peaceful calm in their wake. The six spiritual warriors gathered around her gave thanks and praise to God and His Son for Jeni's deliverance from the anti-Bible spirits. Jeni herself was quiet and leaned against Dee as they left the church arm in arm.

*   *   *

That evening, Jeni and Dee sat once again at the kitchen table. After a quiet moment in the conversation, Jeni looked up as Dee spoke. "Jeni, you should ask the Lord to forgive you for throwing the Bible." Dee suggested.

"I . . . uh . . ." Jeni fought to form the words, her face contorted as she struggled to speak.

"Why don't you just nod yes if I say what you want to pray." Dee offered. Jeni smiled a little in relief and nodded 'yes'. She was so glad Dee seemed to understand.

Jeni bowed her head and shut her eyes for this, her surrogate prayer. "Thank you, Lord, that the nightmares and depression have decreased." Dee said, and Jeni nodded 'yes'. "Thank you, Lord that I can hear Dee's prayers for me, now that I don't 'blank out' so often." Jeni again nodded a strong 'yes'. "Oh God, please forgive me for throwing the Bible and cursing You."

Jeni felt so ashamed. She had been so ugly and filled with bitter frustration, almost hate, on the day she had thrown that temper tantrum. Her head drooped lower, resting on her hands. She did not hate God, though. She did not. She had felt as if He had turned His back on her, and she had wanted to punish Him somehow. But all it had accomplished was that she had punished herself. A faint 'ooh' escaped from the depths of her being before Jeni nodded in the affirmative as tears trickled down through the fingers of the hands which supported her head. She hoped He would forgive her.

"Thank you, Father God, that I can now look at the Bible." Jeni's head suddenly raised off her hands, her shoulders squared as she straightened and nodded 'yes'. As Dee had spoken, Jeni had suddenly realized that God *had* forgiven her. That He did care. And here was the proof. Through His intervention she could, once again, look at His Word. And this time, she would try harder to listen only to His voice and ignore the dark ones.

"In Jesus' name, I pray. Amen." Dee concluded the prayer. Even as Jeni nodded 'yes' her eyes opened. She had a glimmer of a smile and her expression was one of peace. "God knows your thoughts, Jeni. He has heard your prayer." Dee rejoiced with tears in her own eyes. "Oh thank you, Jesus!" Dee paused. "Do you know everything that has just happened, Jeni, or were you 'blanked-out' part of the time?"

Happy tears sprang into Jeni's eyes. "I asked God to forgive me for throwing my Bible and cursing Him," Jeni whispered, unconsciously still nodding 'yes',

"Praise God for no amnesia," Dee said as she reached for the Bible. She laid it once again between them. Jeni looked at it, then looked back up at Dee with joy shining out of her eyes. 'I can see,' her blue eyes shouted silently. "How about trying to read the Bible now?"

Jeni bit her lower lip. It felt like a very big step to her, but she was game to try. "I'll try," she softly said.

Dee opened the Bible to John 15:12 and pointed with her pencil. "Start here," she instructed.

Jeni could see that Dee was praying for her to succeed. With a determined intake of breath, Jeni looked at the Bible. The words were still very difficult to force out, but she would not be defeated. "L . . . love," she stammered, "e . . . e . . . ach o . . . oth . . . other," and she stopped. The dark voices began shouting, pounding at her ever more fiercely with each word she read. As she was beginning to freeze in panic, she felt Dee's warm hand fold over on top of her own.

"Don't listen to the voices. You take control, Jeni." Dee gently encouraged.

Jeni's jaw trembled, then she tightened the muscles. She could do this; she *would* do this. With resolve, she kept her focus on the words before her. "A . . . a . . . as . . . I . . . h . . . h . . . have loved . . . y . . . you." Jeni looked up at Dee in wonder and the beginnings of triumph. She had completed the verse. Dee gave her a great big hug.

Jeni leaned over, hugged Dee back. "It's a war in my head, Dee. When you're telling me one thing, the voices in my head are yelling something else." She rested her head on the older woman's shoulder. "Thank you, Dee."

*　　*　　*

As before, after the stress of the deliverance session Jeni had a few days to relax and soaked up the country air. She found herself smiling much more often then she used to and even laughing. Butch was her frequent shadow; to her own surprise, she even felt happy enough to get involved in games of rough and tumble tug-a-war with him. The evening before she was to go home, Jeni sat on the porch swing and listened to the peepers. If life could be like this, she would not mind living at all. In fact, she was finding she might just downright enjoy it.

The next morning as Dee drove Jeni home, they talked about all the things that had happened and changed since Dee had first invited Jeni into her home. The improvement was significant, but Dee cautioned her that there was almost certain to be more to come. Jeni nodded with a small smile. "I know I still have problems, Dee. But at least now I also have some real hope."

"Do you still have nightmares?" Dee asked.

"Yes, but they aren't nearly as bad," Jeni assured her.

"And the depression?" queried Dee.

"That's better, too," Jeni said with a smile.

"Praise the Lord!" exclaimed Dee. As she stopped the car in front of Jeni's apartment, Dee said, "Give me a call, Jeni, when you're ready to come home with me again." Jeni nodded, gave her friend a smile, then collected her belongings from the car.

CHAPTER 10

Anger and Rebellion

Several weeks had passed before Jeni had asked Dee if it was alright to come out again. Dee listened on the phone as Jeni spoke. "It isn't that I'm wanting to kill myself, Dee. I really am doing better than a few months ago, but, well, I still would really like your help."

Dee immediately responded to the forlorn note in Jeni's voice. "Of course, Jeni. I can pick you up in an hour; is that okay?"

Jeni's voice filled with relief. "Oh, thank you Dee! I'll be waiting!" After hanging up the phone, Dee considered how much demonic activity there still seemed to be. She dialed the church office.

"Pastor Thomson," answered the minister.

"This is Dee. I'll be picking Jeni up today. She's improving, but still having lots of problems. Would you consider having a deliverance session at the church tomorrow?"

"My schedule for the day is full. Would about 8:30 in the evening be all right for you?"

"That would be great!" Dee agreed.

"I'll try to have another pastor and some elders here as well," Pastor Thomson informed Dee.

"Thank you, Jesus," Dee prayed after she had hung up the phone, "for your wonderful, giving people who so willingly put themselves out so that others might be helped."

As she drove to the city for Jeni, Dee prayed for the coming work with Jeni and asked for God's guidance. As her thoughts drifted, she remembered the young lady's understandable frustration and anger at the childhood incest and those that had taken advantage of her. Jeni had also been angered, frustrated and hurt when people accused her of doing things she did not remember. It was only when Jeni had entered therapy that she had come to recognize that there were times when her body did and said things without her own consciousness being in control. These were the times she was 'blanked out'. Dee recalled Jeni telling her that even though she now knew about the blank outs, the knowledge did little to stem the feelings of hurt and betrayal. And that those feelings had led to even more anger. Dee internally looked up toward heaven. *Was this the next step*, she silently asked. Immediately, she felt the warmth of reassurance. It was.

*   *   *

Jeni put her things in the backseat before climbing in beside Dee. It was so good to be in her friend's calming and reassuring presence again. Jeni sighed softly and allowed herself to relax into the passenger seat's upholstery.

As they were driving back to Dee's home, Dee glanced briefly from the road. "Jeni, tell me about the other Christians who had prayed with you and tried to help."

Jeni's muscles stiffened. "Well, you already know some about it." She forced herself to relax. Dee would not dump her like that, she knew it. Dee had not dumped her. Jeni took a deep breath. "There have been several people who have prayed with me and shared scripture with me. Even took me to church sometimes. The next thing I knew, they were mad at me and I never knew why." Jeni's face crumpled in pain. The last time had not been all that long ago, and it had been the worst rejection by far. Steeling herself, Jeni continued.

"This one woman prayed with me and read the Bible to me. She even took me to church with her quite a few times. I thought she was my friend." Jeni could feel the wash of churned emotions all over again. The pain, the betrayal, the shame and the anger. "But then, one day she called to inform me to never call her again or set foot in her church, either. What little hope I had of getting better was dashed. I didn't even know why. I asked, but she wouldn't tell me anything . . . nothing at all."

"How did that make you feel?" Dee asked.

The anger and resentment boiled over and Jeni let them spew out. "Furious!" Jeni blurted out. "Angry at those who encouraged me and then dropped me. Angry with church people, church and God. Angry at His b . . . b . . . book . . . you know."

"Do you mean you're angry at the Bible?"

"Yes, I am," Jeni harshly replied. *They lied! They all lied! What kind of caring was that? What kind of love? And why am I not worth being loved and cared about? Why not!?* A moment of raw emotion shook Jeni's frame. She closed her eyes against it for just a moment, and then went on with the bite still in her voice. "I'm mad at myself, my family too, but especially Granddaddy."

"Are you angry enough to say you're bitter about some things and some people?"

The internal viper bared its fangs in a travesty of a smile. "Hah! You can say that again," Jeni sarcastically declared.

"May I ask you one more question, Jeni?" Dee prompted.

Eyes narrowed and hard, Jeni stared out the window. "Why not," Jeni shrugged her shoulders.

"Do you consider yourself rebellious?"

Dee's question hit Jeni like an unexpected splash of water. Surprised, the anger and pain receded. "Never really thought about it," Jeni said pensively. "Why do you ask?"

"Where one finds anger, there is often rebellion, too," Dee explained.

Jeni sat back, her eyes down. The emotions drained away, allowing her to think. To examine herself as objectively as possible. "Well, I guess I'd have to answer yes. Like smoking, drinking and doing drugs when the doc said not to." With a sigh of resigned recognition, Jeni nodded. "Yeah, I'd say there's been defiance on my part," Jeni admitted to Dee.

"Thank you for your honesty, Jeni. Do you trust me to help you, even if I may not explain things right away?"

Jeni looked over at Dee, the tears beginning to gather in her eyes. "Oh, yes, Dee! Please! Do whatever you think is best. I really need and want your help."

*   *   *

Once they were back at Dee's country home, Jeni busied herself with unpacking and Dee started preparing supper. Dee had skipped lunch and planned to fast for the evening meal as well. She had not told Jeni about the session scheduled at the church.

After supper was over for Jeni and the rest of Dee's family, Dee suggested she and Jeni take a little drive. Jeni was herself until the church came into view . . . then the demons took over. After pulling into the church's parking lot, Dee had to coax and cajole and even do some pulling and pushing to get a very reluctant Jeni out of the car and walking toward the door and inside. The pastors and elders were patiently awaiting the arrival of the two women. They, too, had prepared for this meeting by fasting and praying.

As a group, they guided the stiff young woman to a pew. Once Jeni was seated, Pastor Thomson prayed. "Father God, we're

gathered here to minister to the spiritual needs of this young lady.
We ask for your guidance. We thank you for the authority and
power through your Son, Jesus, and your Word. In Jesus' name we
pray. Amen."

Pastor Stafford read James 5: 14 and 15 out loud. "Is any one
of you sick? He should call the elders of the church to pray over
him and anoint him with oil in the name of the Lord." He opened
a tiny bottle with olive oil in it and put some on Jeni's forehead.
"Dear Lord, we have anointed Jeni with oil as your Word says and
we are asking for her spiritual healing." Again he read from the
Bible. "And the prayer offered in faith will make the sick person
well; the Lord will raise him up. If he has sinned he will be forgiven."
He paused before continuing. "Jeni, if you would like Jesus in
your life, repeat after me. Dear Jesus, I am a sinner . . ."

The demons had control; Jeni had been sitting deathly still,
completely unresponsive and her eyes staring out into nothingness.
When Pastor Stafford had started the prayer, however, Jeni jerked
into motion. Her body struggled to get up out of the pew and flee,
attempting to pull away from the hands that gently but firmly held
her. The team held her physically, as they also upheld her in prayer.

In three different intervals, Reverend Stafford recalled the
scriptures of Colossians 3: 8 and Ephesians 4: 26 and 31. He
rebuked the demons of anger against those who had hurt Jeni:
demons of anger with her family and demons of anger toward
God's people. Next he rebuked the demons of anger against God's
church. With each rebuke, the evil spirits being specifically rebuked
fought the team. Each group of spirits attempted to bang Jeni's
head against the back of the pew, use her own hands to choke her
in a vise-like grip and claw her face. Finally, in each case as the
demonic spirits were forced to leave her, Jeni's body was racked
with deep, painful coughing.

The team took a break while Dee stayed with Jeni as she sat,
unresponsive and still, on the pew. After a short while, the staunch
team members gathered again. During the second part of the
deliverance session, Reverend Stafford read Isaiah 30:1 and First
Samuel 12:15 out loud and rebuked the various demons of

rebellion. First he addressed those demonic spirits of rebellion against God. He then rebuked the spirits of rebellion against the Bible. Lastly, he addressed the demonic spirits of rebellion against Jesus. As each set of demons were rebuked, the responses were once again very similar. When any part of the team relaxed their protective hold on her, Jeni would immediately try to get to her feet to run. As the these spirits were rebuked, there was also a look of untold fear in her eyes and eventually Jeni would droop as if unconscious.

It was about three hours before the rebuking was finished and Jeni's 'blank out' had passed. Although she had no memory of what had happened, her own personality was back in control. As she drove herself and the exhausted young lady back to her home, Dee shook her head slightly in amazement. *She must have had hundreds of demons within her.*

*   *   *

Jeni was so tired when they got back to the house that she went straight to bed. The next morning after Dee's son, John, had gone to his classes and Harv had set off to work, the two women once again sat together at the kitchen table for morning devotions. Afterwards, they sat talking for a little while.

"Do you remember what happened last night, Jeni?"

"Not a thing," Jeni said with an apologetic shake of her head and shrug.

"First we cast out demons of anger. Actually, several categories of them. Those of anger with family, with God's people and those of anger against his church." Dee unconsciously shook her head at the memory of the evening before. "Then there were those spirits of anger with God, and ones who were of anger with the Bible and then finally, those who were of anger against Jesus."

Dee rubbed a hand absently along her jaw. "It was a long evening," Dee continued. "We had a fifteen minute break and then separately rebuked the demons of rebellion. Those of rebellion against God, the ones of rebellion against the Bible and lastly the spirits of rebellion against Jesus."

"Do you suppose that is why I feel so much better this morning?"

Dee smiled. "Could be!" Her dark eyes sparkled and she gave Jeni's hand an encouraging squeeze.

"I'm having some better times at home, too," Jeni added. "I actually even find myself laughing, sometimes!" Jeni smiled at Dee and gave her hand a squeeze back. Butch came over and nuzzled Jeni's other hand.

Dee laughed and said, "Looks like someone would like your attention."

Jeni smiled and pushed away from the table. "I think we'll go for a walk." Jeni motioned to the dog who was watching her with pricked ears. "Come on, Butch! Let's take a walk, boy." Jeni giggled at his eagerness as they went toward the front door. "You've got me for two more days, doggy. Let's make the most of them." They happily set off down the road together.

Over the next two days, Dee was pleased to note how often Jeni was able to smile and even laugh. The lines of tension around the younger woman's eyes and mouth had softened as she had been able to relax more and more. As she watched, Dee lifted her heart up in praise and gratitude. What could be more rewarding than seeing broken wings being mended through God's love and strength?

CHAPTER 11

Self Mutilation

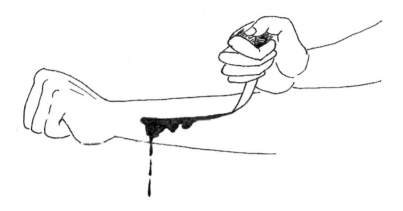

J eni stared into the mirror, glaring at the beautiful young lady with the golden hair who glared back at her. *Why do they always look at you and never at me?* She turned away and flung herself into a chair kicking out at anything that presented itself. *They look at the outside wrapper, but do they care? All they care about is, 'oh, so pretty'. Do they care about me? No! They don't care. They don't even care enough to get to know me . . . the me inside. They don't want to be bothered.*

If no one else cares, then why should I?

Jeni slouched in the chair, her head propped up on a fist. *Ow, my stomach hurts.* She held both sides of her tummy tenderly. *The voices were horrible last night, calling me dirty names, using foul language and demanding that I get my razor blades. I don't remember anything else, but now my belly is all cut up! How could I have done this?* She glared at the phone as it began ringing. Two rings, then three, then four. Finally, after she had lost count, she picked up the handset. "Hello," she said with an exasperated sigh.

"Hello, Jeni, this is Dee. I was just thinking of you as I noticed the buds coming out on the trees in the woods. I wondered how you were doing."

Jeni sat silent for a moment. "Okay, I guess," she said, only half-heartedly trying to keep the surliness out of her voice.

Dee hesitated a brief moment. "Would you like to come for a visit?"

Some part of Jeni reached for the help her friend was offering her. "Yeah, sure."

*   *   *

Jeni was silent and withdrawn as she climbed in the car for a few more days in the country. Spring was coming. Buds were on the bushes and trees. Even a few jonquils had begun to bud and in places the crocus were open and drinking in the returning sun. Dee looked over at her passenger, concerned. Jeni did not seem to notice that Spring was in the air. Dee made several comments, inviting a conversation, but Jeni merely grunted or simply sat silent.

As they entered the house, Dee made an open, sweeping gesture. "Make yourself at home, Jeni. I'll go make some lunch for us." Dee went to the kitchen to prepare lunch for the two of them. Just as she was ready to tell Jeni that lunch was on the table, the sounds of feet running through the house and the banging of the screen door reached Dee's ears. The older woman looked out the window in time to see Jeni disappear into the woods. Dee's concern for Jeni deepened, and she breathed a prayer. *Lord, please help Jeni, and please show me how I can help her.*

Twenty minutes later Jeni returned, cradling her left wrist in her right hand. Dee met her in the front entranceway. Her searching eyes noticed the blood as Jeni closed the door. She reached for Jeni's hand. "Let me see," Dee stated as matter-of-factly as any other nurse. Recognizing a razor-like cut, Dee was relieved that it was not deep and did not need stitches. Taking Jeni into the bathroom to the first aid cabinet, Dee disinfected the area and bandaged the surface wound. "Why Jeni? Why did you do this?" Dee asked, puzzled.

Jeni twitched and looked away. "I didn't mean to . . ."

"You're not being straight with me, young lady," Dee said as she led Jeni to the room she occupied when visiting. "Now, give me the razor," she demanded.

"You're mad at me," Jeni whined. "I can't help what I do when I'm blanked out."

Dee's eyes sharpened on Jeni. "*Give me the razor!*" Dee emphatically stated.

Jeni reached over the rumpled bed covers and pulled them down, revealing the razor blade. She picked it up and handed it to Dee.

"Are there anymore?"

"No," Jeni flinched ever so slightly, " . . . honest," Jeni hesitantly replied.

Lord, Dee prayed, *Is this more deceit? Are there more razor blades? Did she know what she was doing? Please guide me.* Aloud she directed, "Let's go have lunch." She led the way to the kitchen where Jeni mainly pushed the food on her plate around with her fork, only eating a few bites.

Food and dishes put aside, Dee opened a conversation, "I don't believe you were 'blanked out' when you did this. I want to know why. What is your reasoning?" Her eyes were firmly focused on Jeni's face, but without accusation.

Slowly and softly Jeni answered, "It calms my tensions and depression." She looked down and to one side.

"Why did you run out of the house like something was after you, if it calms you and makes you less depressed?" Jeni's shoulder muscles tightened, hunching them inward. After a moment she shrugged. Dee continued, "Did it calm you?"

"Not really," Jeni admitted slowly.

"Have you done this before?"

"Yes." Jeni sighed and pulled her long sleeve shirt above her elbow, revealing the many scars she carried with her every day.

Dee did not allow herself to react at the sight. "Where did you get the idea that cutting yourself would relieve your tension?"

"Everybody knows that," Jeni attempted to convince Dee.

Dee's lips compressed slightly. "Listen to me, Jeni, where did you get the idea that cutting yourself would help?" Now apparently indifferent, the young lady simply shrugged her shoulders. Dee pressed further. "Do you remember that you promised to be totally honest with me if I would promise to help you?"

"Yes," Jeni replied reluctantly.

"You're not being totally honest with me."

With irritation, Jeni retorted, "And you expect too much from me!"

Calmly, Dee reminded her, "Before we started working together for your deliverance, I agreed to try on one condition . . . that you would be honest with me 100% of the time. You agreed to this, but you haven't been totally honest with me. I have given you the last several months of my time and energy, fasting, studying, praying and ministering to you in one way or another. You need to decide now whether or not I continue working with you. I will not continue without 100% cooperation from you."

Dee paused before continuing. "Do you remember the story in Acts 5: 1—11? About Ananias and Saphira, when they lied to Peter?"

"Yes."

"You need to realize the seriousness of lying to God's servant, and in your case, at this time, I am God's servant."

Jeni rose from the table and strode to her room, her head held high and her eyes cold. Dee prayed as she cleared the table and put a roast on to slow-cook. Occasionally she thought she heard sobbing. Dee's spirit reached out at the plight of this young lady and she felt as if her own heart were breaking. "Oh Lord, only you can rectify the situation and her life. God, help us." Dee sobbed as tears splashed onto the cook pot lid. She was still puttering about the kitchen when Jeni entered carrying a book.

"I am sorry, Dee," she said meekly as she handed her mentor a book along with more razor blades. "This book says, 'cutting oneself is a method of relieving tension'."

"Thank you, Jeni. Where did you get this book?"

"At the bookstore in the mall a few days ago." Her eyes dropped. "I have to tell you something else." Now Jeni hesitated.

"Go on," Dee encouraged.

"I started reading it when I got home from the store . . . The next thing I knew, it was the next day and my stomach hurt. When I looked at my belly, it was . . . like this." She raised her shirt, showing that she was cut from one side to the other, sick words and words of profanity. "Honestly, I have no memory of doing this. **Please** don't give up on me!" Jeni looked into Dee's eyes for a moment, then looked downward again. "Um . . . But . . . Well, I do remember cutting myself today. I'm sorry for lying to you."

"Thank you, Jeni for telling me. I know it wasn't easy for you."

"Will you forgive me?" Jeni meekly asked.

"Of course," said Dee, giving her a little hug.

*   *   *

Jeni sat in the living room with a book on her lap, but her eyes and her thoughts were lost far away. *I know that Dee cares about me. Even when she is stern, it is because she cares. I know that Carol cares, too. And the pastors that are working with Dee to help me. They care. So why, oh why do I still sometimes want to give up and die?*

As a tear slowly wended its way down her cheek, a voice answered her. Calm, deep, and totally unlike anything that she was used to hearing in her head, the voice whispered to her, *They care. But you must also care; you must care about yourself. Just as I care about you.*

Jeni bowed her head. Somewhere inside her, a giant crevasse of emptiness seemed to begin filling up, and Jeni began crying in earnest.

*   *   *

During the afternoon, Dee called the pastor to set up an appointment for a deliverance session the next day at the church. After supper, the two women remained at the table. Dee read to Jeni from the Bible, choosing the account of Ananias and Saphira and again emphasizing her demand for absolute honesty from Jeni.

Jeni nodded from time to time as she listened intently, her eyes focused on Dee's face. "I had some trouble hearing with the voices so loud, but I understand what you read and why. And I didn't blank out either!" Jeni said.

"Let's pray," Dee said and bowed her head only to hear choking and gurgling sounds. She looked up to see a contorted face. "I rebuke you anti-prayer demon in the name of Jesus and by the power of his blood. Leave her, NOW!"

Jeni suddenly slumped forward for an instant before she caught herself and straightened back up. Her face was relaxed now and she was able to look into Dee's eyes, which she could not do a few minutes earlier when the evil spirits were dominating her. "Thank you, Jesus," Dee prayed out loud. "Keep control of your mind, Jeni,. Be strong and ignore the voices. Now, try to say 'Jesus'."

Jeni tightened her internal focus and fought to make her mouth work. "J . . . Je . . . sus" Jeni stammered.

"Again and again, please," Dee urged as she rebuked the evil spirits as Jeni successfully said 'Jesus' several times without facial distortions or stuttering.

"You did it!" Dee exclaimed. "You did it! Praise the Lord!"

Jeni smiled at Dee. "And thank you, too, Dee. Without you, I would have never have known how much He really cares about me. I would have given up."

                    *   *   *

Taking Jeni to church the next day was a breeze compared to the earlier trip. She was able to walk to the car and get into it without any difficulty, displaying any resistance or indications of 'blanking out'. After Dee had parked the car in the church parking lot, Jeni was able to get out and and walk halfway to the church door. Only then did she lose control, but even then, she merely turned as if to walk back to the car. With comparative ease, Dee directed her back toward the church, holding her hand. They entered and Dee led her to the front pew where the pastors and elders were waiting.

The two sets of evil spirits that were addressed this day were self—mutilation and suicide. The deliverance session was similar to what the team had already experienced; the demonic manifestations that session included trying to run away, the vise-like grip of her hands compressing her trachea, heavy perspiration, choking, and finally coughing. The team members were ready for each type of manifestation, however, so there were no outstanding problems. Jeni's own personality was soon back in control of her body again; the demons which had been addressed that day had been cast out.

That evening after supper, Dee and Jeni took their accustomed places at the kitchen table. Dee started with prayer. "Thank you, Lord God, for the continued improvement in Jeni. We thank you for each demon that has been cast out. We recognize that there have been many and there still are some, so Father, please keep your protective hand over her until she is totally free to worship you in Spirit and in truth—until she is able to follow her present desire to be your obedient child. In Jesus' name, we pray. Amen."

Then Dee assisted Jeni in reading from the Bible, "Leviticus 19: 28. Do not cut your bodies . . ." and "Exodus 20:13. You shall not murder." Jeni was pleased and a little relieved at how much easier it was to read God's Word.

That night and over the next couple of days, Jeni thought often about how hurting herself through cutting or trying to kill herself was a form of expressing her own inability to care about herself. She remembered how often she had wanted to hurt those who had hurt her by causing them grief, how often she had imagined their remorse at her death. In remembering, Jeni suddenly began to realize that the hideous accusatory and demanding voices seemed to always precede the times when she was swamped with the extreme depths of despair and the hopelessness that lead to her self-destructive actions and the blank outs.

Surrounded in the supportive atmosphere of Dee's home, Jeni finally began to reach a much deeper understanding. She began to realize that because she had not felt worthy of being cared about by others, she had come to the conclusion somewhere deep inside that she should not care about herself, either. This had been followed by anger and deliberate rebellion. It was that concept of worthlessness which had been a crack in her soul . . . and she wondered if perhaps it had been that crack which had allowed the darkness to enter from the inside, even as some people had hurt her and brought darkness to her from the outside.

Now, she knew beyond a doubt that God loved her. He showed it to her through the Bible, Dee, Harv, the ministry team and her mom. She just had not been able to see it before. "I am a worthwhile human being," she declared to Butch, who responded with a big wet kiss.

CHAPTER 12

God Is Greater

A s Dee pulled up in front of Jeni's apartment, Jeni smiled
and waved from the sidewalk. "Hi, Dee. I'm ready to go!"
"Is that a knitting bag you have there?" Dee asked.

"Yep," Jeni answered with a smile. "Or maybe a crocheting
bag," she giggled as she pulled out an afghan she was crocheting.

"It's nice to see you smile. And the afghan is very pretty," Dee
said as her eyes crinkled at the corners. She was encouraged and
pleased to see how stable and happy Jeni was at the beginning of
one of her visits. On prior visits, Dee had generally only seen the
bright side of Jeni after a deliverance session.

The trip went fast and Jeni was soon settling her things into the guest room. As she came out of the room, she found Butch waiting for her. His dark eyes gazed at her imploringly and he wagged his tail in hope. Jeni smiled and reached down to pat his head. "Dee," she called, "Butch and I are off for a walk." With a spring in both of their steps, they went out the front door. As Jeni turned onto the dirt road, Butch ran up and down and circled around beside her. When she came back, she presented Dee with a lovely bunch of wildflowers she had picked, and she chattered with enthusiasm about the wonderful weather and the things she had seen.

That evening Dee took Jeni to the church for another deliverance session. This time, the young lady was able to walk from the car and into the church before she spaced out. Pastor Thomson greeted them and led Jeni to the front pew where she sat down. Everyone took their places surrounding her. After a brief prayer, the spirit of incest was addressed. "In Jesus' name and by the power of His blood *leave her, now!*" Jeni's hands went to her face in a flash and her fingers with their long nails became claws, scraping her skin from the upper cheeks to her jaws and raising long welts on her face. The deliverance team scrambled to catch her hands and wrists again, anchoring them firmly so that no more damage was done. They had not been sufficiently prepared for the speed and strength with which the demonic spirits had reacted. Once Jeni was firmly held again, the team members looked at each other with chagrin. Much more care was given from then on to protect her from the angry spirits being cast out.

The next spirit commanded to leave was the spirit of rape, and then, with First Corinthians 6: 9 in mind, the spirit of promiscuous sex. With no prior knowledge of such an experience, Dee heard herself address the spirit of lesbianism, as described in Leviticus 18: 22 and Romans 1: 24-27 and 32. Jeni's muscles strained to run with each spirit cast out, but the pressure on her shoulders and knees kept her seated in the pew. Her head was held to prevent it from any gyrating. However, she became rigid and squealed and coughed as each one of these spirits left her. A few moments after this set of exorcisms was completed, Jeni raised her head and looked at Dee with a peaceful expression.

The team relaxed and broke apart as people made their way to the bathrooms and the coffee urn. Fifteen minutes later they were all in place again and ready to start the next step.

The final set of demonic spirits called upon and rebuked were the those of the occult. The team separately rebuked the spirits of spell casting, the ouija board, spiritism, and witchcraft. The manifestations were similar to the previous sessions, except this time there was no squealing or rigidity although there was heavy perspiration. After the final group of spirits had been addressed and cast out, everyone relaxed and chatted a few minutes. Jeni mustered a smile and said 'thank you' to the team. She and Dee left arm in arm, Jeni leaning slightly on the older woman for support.

There was not much evening left when the two of them got home, but the next morning they took their places at the kitchen table.

"I had the best night's sleep that I've had in a long time, years even," Jeni declared with a smile. "Each time I come here, I get better." A thoughtful and slightly puzzled look went across her face. "You know, though, something strange happened at the church while I was blanked out," Jeni continued.

"Yes?" questioned Dee.

"I saw the spirits of Granddaddy and Derrick and Pamela. They showed themselves and then floated away, one at a time."

"Who is Pamela?" Dee asked.

"She was my case worker for awhile when I was a kid. She told me she needed to have sex with me so I would be better emotionally. I never liked it and I've never liked it with men either."

Wow! Dee thought. *Thank you, Lord,* she prayed silently in thanksgiving for the Holy Spirit's leading the evening before. "Well, Jeni, last night we rebuked the spirits of incest, rape and lesbianism. It sounds as if it was those spirits you saw as they were forced to leave." Both women sat quietly for a few moments before Dee continued. "What do you think about witchcraft and the occult?" Dee asked Jeni.

"I'm not sure," Jeni responded. "I was intrigued by it in high school and read a lot about it. Some of my friends and I tried the ouija board and casting spells and stuff. When I saw that movie, 'The Exorcist', it sort of turned me off. It was even more scary than back in high school."

"I am glad it did turn you off," Dee replied. "We also cast out occult spirits last night." She read several scriptures to Jeni about these activities, including Leviticus 19: 31 and 20: 6, Deuteronomy 18: 9-12, Isaiah 8:19 and Galatians 5:19-21. Dee showed her in God's Word that He had forbidden the occult.

"Oh," said Jeni thoughtfully. "I hadn't known that."

Dee reached for the Bible and turned to James 4: 7, then she pushed the open Bible in front of Jeni. "Submit yourselves then to God. R-resist the devil, and he will flee from you," Jeni was able to read with very little trouble.

"That's great Jeni! Do you still have to battle with the voices?"

"Yes, but not as much as I used to have to." Jeni's smile clouded over a bit as her brows drew together. "Dee, may I ask you about something?"

"Sure thing, ask away."

"Well, at home I went to find the Bible that Mom gave me; I wanted to try to read a little of it. I really had to look for awhile to find it." She hesitated for a brief moment. "When I opened it, the voices were so loud, I started to get queasy, so I yelled, 'I rebuke you!' That's all I remember until the blanking out passed." Jeni's hands gripped each other. "Dee," she continued, visibly shaken, "when I came to myself I was on Main Street in the middle of the road near the hospital, and an ambulance was coming straight at me. The siren was on. The red lights were flashing and that awful horn was blasting. I could have been hit!"

Jeni looked over at Dee with concern on her face. "I rarely blank out anymore, and if I do it's only for a few minutes. What happened, Dee?"

"Praise the Lord that you weren't hit. I can understand why you are wondering why you blanked out," Dee replied. Jeni nodded. Dee continued. "You have spent a number of years in disobedience to God, and you haven't made it all the way back to

Him yet. The devil knows you're becoming free from him and closer to God. He doesn't want to let you go. Hang on to the promises God made in James 4: 7. Just continue to 'Submit yourself to God, resist the devil and he will flee from you'. Until you are totally free from the evil spirits, the devil can still control you, sometimes. Jesus gave the ability and authority to rebuke the demons to his disciples but not to everybody. It tells us about this in Luke 9: 1 and Luke 10: 17 and 19"

"But, I'm getting there, aren't I," she had asked in much need of encouragement.

"I believe you are," said Dee. "What do you think?"

"I don't blank out very often anymore and if I do, it's not for days, just minutes or hours at the most. I'm not depressed. I've not cut myself or thought of suicide since I was here last. And I haven't had any nightmares since my last visit, either."

"That's really great," Dee responded. "Praise the Lord!"

"There is still one problem, Dee."

"Okay," Dee encouraged, "Tell me about it."

"I still can't pray by myself. I tried and I got zonked. I blanked out, but it didn't last long."

"Jeni, I'm sure that God hears deaf mutes when they talk to him silently. Why don't you try praying silently when you're home alone."

"Okay, I'll try that," Jeni said with a smile.

*   *   *

That afternoon Jeni went outside to the porch to sit, crochet and think. She felt the need to mull over what Dee had told her. She had felt like she had lost herself when those people had forced her into sex. She shuddered as she realized that for her at least, losing that possession of herself had apparently opened a door and allowed something else to creep in. With a grimace, she did admit to herself that she had added to the problem. After high school she had encouraged some guys, preferring to have sex rather than to have no attention from them. Those drug parties had also been filled with bad situations, not to mention what the drugs had done to her already precarious health. She was so thankful that God, through His people, had forced those horrid things back out of her.

As she continued to crochet and think, she mentally turned over the scriptures that Dee had read her that morning about the occult and witchcraft. She had never thought about where the power they tapped into might come from. She had never thought about whether or not it was from God or from Satan. Jeni shook her head sadly as she bent over and scratched Butch's ears. She doubted whether the other kids had ever thought about it either. *Why didn't they teach us in Sunday School that the ouija board game and tarot cards were Satan's playthings? Why did they have the books on witchcraft in the school library? I shouldn't have tried to cast those spells at home. No wonder I got queezy when Tom wanted to cast a bad spell on the teacher. Sure glad I didn't get more involved in that witchcraft stuff than I did.* She sighed, seeing her experiences in that area as yet another open door for demons to walk through.

Then she smiled. "Well, Butch, I am getting better. Dee has helped me find that barrier that Carol and I had been looking for for so long. And better yet, Dee and the others are helping remove those barriers, one by one. We won't let Satan or his demons win, will we, boy?" Butch yipped and danced in a circle. Jeni could not help but laugh. "Alright," she said. Putting her needlework to one side, she motioned Butch forward. "Another walk before dinner won't hurt either one of us." Jeni's laugh was clear and untroubled as the two of them set off down the road.

*   *   *

As usual, Jeni enjoyed a couple of relaxing days in the country before Dee drove her back to her city apartment. "Just remember," Dee told Jeni as the car moved past the fields on their way back to the city, "Like it says in John 10: 29, God is the greatest, with more power than Satan. He's brought you a long way back to Himself. Just keep looking to Him. He'll see you to victory."

"I won't forget, Dee. How could I?" Jeni gave her friend a large smile. "He sent you, so I know He really does care about me, even though I was mad at Him. And I know He's helping me, through you and the others."

After Dee had pulled in at the curb, Jeni got out of the car and gathered up her luggage from the backseat. Then she went around to the driver's side and motioned for Dee to roll down the window. With a big smile, Jeni handed Dee an envelope. "This is for you. Read it after you get home." She squeezed Dee's hand a moment, then turned away. "Love ya," she called as she reached the steps and blew Dee a kiss. With a grin, she scampered up the stairs.

Once Dee was home, she pulled open the envelope. Inside, she found Jeni's grateful tribute, "Dee, My Special Friend." Tears sparkled on her lashes as she sat still and silent, thanking God for guiding her in helping this lovely young woman.

*   *   *

Dee, My Special Friend

There was nowhere to turn
I'd exhausted all leads
I prayed over and over
Dear God, take me please.

Then a few months ago
Wishing for my life to end
Though I barely knew you
You were there as my friend.
He surely had a reason
For me to reach out
He led me to call, though
My heart was filled with doubt.

I was oh, so afraid
And filled with despair
I thought my life was done
Beyond all hope and repair.
Then you loved and you cared

When I felt unworthy of love
You reached out to me
With His help from above.

And I started to believe
You told me it was so
There is hope for me
The enemy has to let go.

I love you so much
For letting Him use you
To help us fight this battle
Until it is through.

A special person you are
So precious to me
You've given so much of yourself
So that I can be free.

I know there's coming a day
I'll be set totally free
Because you and God
Didn't give up on me.

I look forward to the day
We can worship together
With praises and songs
To Him, forever and ever.

                                        Love, Jeni

CHAPTER 13

Victory

J eni waited impatiently for Dee's car to come around the corner. She had been thinking about this for a while now, and she really wanted to talk to Dee about it. Jeni knew how far she had been able to go on her own, and how far she had been able to go with therapy and medication. Jeni grimaced slightly as she remembered the days, the weeks, the years, of being swamped by the bitter darkness that kept trying to drag her into the irredeemable pits.

She had tried so hard, and so had Carol, but she had never been able to climb high enough to feel the light without once again slipping back into the darkness. Back then, she had relied on human wisdom and knowledge to help her. Now, she knew the truth. That might get you so far, but never far enough.

It had been close to a year since Dee started ministering to Jeni. With Dee as her guide and mentor, she had recently seen that the only true answer was to rely on God's wisdom and power to help her and save her. Jeni knew, beyond any doubt, that what had made such a difference in her life had been Dee's discernment of the spiritual battles within her and the willingness and commitment that Dee had made to see her released from the bondage of the demons she had not even known had taken up residence within her.

Jeni squeaked in excitement as she saw Dee's car turn onto her street. Quickly, she gathered her luggage and bundled herself and it through the apartment door. With a grin, she bounded down the stairs and met Dee's car at the curb. Almost as soon as she was safely in, she turned to Dee to make the request that she had been thinking of practically non-stop. "Dee, many Christians have tried to help me," Jeni began as Dee guided the car through the city streets. "They prayed with me and some took me to church with them. Each time this happened, I would get a little better. But then they'd lose interest or something and stop, and I would never know why. After they would stop seeing me, I'd get as bad as ever, maybe even worse." Jeni paused for a moment to gather herself. This was very important to her.

"Since you and those you've taken me to have been helping me, I feel almost normal. I've been thinking about this a lot. I wish you would write a book, so other Christians would know what to do to help others like me. I'm sure there are other people who are trapped by drugs, witchcraft, sexual sins and the like, who can't free themselves, that have opened the door for Satan's forces to take over and ruin their lives."

"I'll think about it." Dee said. Jeni watched Dee's face for a moment. With a sigh, she acknowledged that Dee was not as enthusiastic about the idea as she had hoped, but she rather surprisingly found that she trusted everything would work out for the best.

After a pause, Dee changed the direction of the conversation. "There have already been many evil spirits cast out, but unless you pray regularly and read God's word (or listen to it on tape), more demons can inhabit you again. The scripture tells us about that in Luke 11:24-26. But as long as you are God's child, truly serving Him and doing the things he has told us to do, you don't need to worry about the demons coming back. God is greater than the devil himself."

"I'm able to pray whenever I want to now," Jeni volunteered with a smile. "I just pray silently, Dee, and it works."

"Hey, that's wonderful!" Dee was also smiling now.

Jeni grinned back. "And I can listen to Christian music, too, without the voices tormenting me."

"What about the Bible?" Dee inquired.

"That's still hard to do, but I can read a short verse or two without any blank outs." Jeni smiled to herself. *It is so much more than I have been able to do for years. Thank you, Jesus, for your help and your people.*

Dee began to sing. "Victory in Jesus," and Jeni joined her on the next phrase, "My Savior forever." They both broke out in laughter. This was a very special moment for both of them.

*   *   *

When she had picked Jeni up again, Dee had been so pleased. It was wonderful to see her happy and able to exchange conversation with ease, even be talkative. Dee was not as certain about Jeni's request, however. Dee was not really a writer, although she had done some writing when she had felt impressed to by the Lord. The thought of writing Jeni's story was daunting. She would not even know where to begin.

The next morning they headed off to church for a very special session. Jeni got into the car with eager anticipation for continued improvement. On the way to church, she repeated the request she had made before. "Dee, please write a book about my problems and how God has delivered me, so that others may be helped also."

Dee could hear Jeni's sincere wish to help others. Reminding herself that God would guide her if it was His will, this time, Dee responded, "I'll pray about it."

At the church, Jeni walked into the building without prodding or blanking out and sat herself in the now familiar pew. As the team was greeting Jeni, Dee spoke to Pastor Thomson. "When I pray about any further rebuking of demons, all that comes to mind is unnecessary medication." Dee was aware that Jeni had misused her medications at times, although she did not think Jeni had recently.

"I had that same impression today," the pastor concurred. They joined the others in the sanctuary. After prayer, Dee rebuked the spirits of unnecessary medication. Jeni coughed mildly, then looked up at Dee and smiled.

At that point Pastor Thomson inquired of Jeni, "Have you asked God to forgive you for all you have done that was displeasing to Him, Jeni?"

"Some things," Jeni said thoughtfully, "but I'm sure I don't even remember them all."

He inquired further, "Would you like to?"

"Oh yes," Jeni responded in all sincerity.

"Would you like to ask Christ into your life to be your Savior?"

"Yes, oh yes," Jeni replied enthusiastically.

Remembering Jeni's previous inability to pray, Pastor Thomson suggested, "If I say what you would like to say, you repeat it. If you have any trouble repeating what I say, and you are praying it in your head, just say yes in agreement. Any questions?"

"No, I'm ready."

"Dear Jesus," he began, "I am a sinner and sorry for my sins."

"Jesus, I am so sorry," Jeni sighed as a tear rolled down her cheek.

Pastor Thomson continued, "I believe you died for me. Come into my life and be my Savior."

"Be my Savior." Jeni sobbed.

Dee slipped her a tissue as Pastor Thomson said, "Amen." And there was a chorus of "Amens." One of the elders put a small tray with some broken pieces of unleavened bread in front of Jeni. Remembering the procedure from her childhood, she took a piece. Reading Matthew 26: 26 through 28, and Mark 14: 22 through 24, Pastor Thomson said, " . . . Jesus took bread, gave thanks and broke it, and gave it to his disciples, saying, 'Take and eat; this is my body.'"

Jeni remembered these words of Jesus from her childhood and put the bread in her mouth as another tear rolled down her cheek. The elders handed her a tiny cup of grape juice and Pastor Thomson read, "Then he [Jesus] took the cup, gave thanks and offered it to them, saying, 'Drink from it, all of you. This is my blood of the covenant, which is poured out for many for the forgiveness of sins'."

Jeni drank the juice. "Thank you, Jesus," she said softly.

Pastor Thomson reached out his hand in fellowship, which Jeni warmly received. Her big smile was a joy to behold as she thanked each one of the ministry team personally. Jeni was thrilled and with more strength than ususal gave Dee a big hug which almost took Dee's breath away.

Shortly afterwards, she and Dee once again left the church arm in arm, singing "Amazing Grace" together. Jeni was totally free!

Arriving back at the country home, Jeni bent down and swooped Butch up into her arms. "Hey, Butch, I'm so happy! I gave my life to Jesus." It must have sounded good to the little dog, because he gave her a sloppy doggie kiss right on the lips. Jeni wiped her mouth, laughing as she put him down and went to the kitchen to help Dee prepare their meal.

The two ladies thoroughly enjoyed one another's company the next couple of days. Jeni was even relaxed enough that Harv joined them for their evening devotions.

The trip back to Jeni's apartment was indeed a cheerful one with the young woman chatting about her new found life. "It really is great to be alive," she volunteered. "I'm certainly looking forward to each day, now."

"That's just wonderful, Jeni," Dee exclaimed as they arrived at the apartment. "Keep in touch," Dee called as she watched Jeni ascend the steps.

*   *   *

A few days later, Jeni awoke not feeling well at all. She took her morning medication and sat at the table to have breakfast, but she was so woozy, she called her mother instead. "Mom," her speech was slow and slurred, "I don't feel well. I'm so . . . ."

"Jeni!" Cindy called out. Then she heard a thud. She ran for her cell phone and called the emergency number for Jeni's area, begging them to check on her daughter.

"Ma'am," the officer on the scene later said on the phone to Cindy. "They are transporting your daughter to City Hospital."

Upon her arrival, Jeni was taken to the Emergency Room. "Wake up, wake up," called the physician. Jeni roused a little. "What do we have here, an overdose of something?"

"No," Jeni spoke faintly. She was going to explain that she did not do drugs anymore, just her medications, but she fell back asleep.

The doctor ordered blood work to be done and Jeni was admitted to the hospital. Through the blood testing, the hospital staff found that she no longer needed the psychiatric medications. In fact this latest crisis had been caused by her prescribed medication, even though she had taken it as directed. The doctor immediately removed her from the medication.

Then, something Jeni had never thought to see happened. A few months after the pyschotropic medicines were removed, she was at the mental health center, waiting for her weekly session with Carol. After Carol had collected her from the waiting room and motioned her into her office, Jeni was surprised to see Carol lean against the edge of her desk.

"Jeni," Carol began, "I have something I want to ask you."

Jeni looked at her therapist with some trepidation. Carol's voice told her that whatever this was, it was big. "Okay."

Carol smoothed her jaw with a hand before beginning. "You have shown a marked improvement over this past year. I have absolutely no records of any crises you precipitated for over ten months. Your doctor removed the psychiatric drugs several months ago, and you remain stable. And here, in therapy, we seem to have worked through every residual issue from your past." Carol smiled. "So, here is my question. Do you feel that you still need therapy?"

Jeni sat stunned. She had been in therapy for so long that the possibility of not needing it had not occurred to her. Carol smiled warmly at her. "I know that this may be a surprise to you. We can continue if you feel you need to, and of course, any time you feel you need to come back . . . maybe just for a little support . . . you can."

Jeni looked up at Carol, shaking her head in amazement, her mouth stretched in a large smile. "Oh, Carol. I have wanted so much to tell you, over and over again, how much you have meant to me. Without your help, I would never have made it as long as I did in that darkness." Jeni spontaneously jumped up and hugged her therapist. "But I have found that the help I really had to have was God's help. Without His help, I wasn't able to use the help that you offered. With His help, finally everything you had been telling me was able to lock into place."

Jeni wiped the moisture from her eyes. "You have been the very best, Carol. But I think you're right. I guess I don't think I need therapy anymore." Jeni grinned and threw her hands wide, "Thank you, Carol." *And thank you, Lord Jesus!*

When Jeni got home, she called Dee with the news that they had discontinued the counseling. Dee told her over the phone how much she marveled that during that one year of special ministry, God had given this young lady emotional stability . . . and this after fourteen years of mental health hospitalizations, counseling, and psychiatric medications. Both of them chattered like schoolgirls, thrilled and praising God about Jeni's new life.

*　　*　　*

Not long afterwards, Jeni moved to an apartment building compatible to her needs due to her physical disabilities. The systemic lupus had progressed in its muscular and balance effects to the point that she could no longer safely go up and down stairs. Quite soon her beautiful face and radiant personality became a joy for others in the building. Over the phone Jeni told Dee, "I love to bake and give it away, Dee, and I crochet slippers, pillows and afghans to give away. Some of the ladies call me 'angel'." Jeni giggled. "Neat, huh?"

"Sure is," agreed Dee. "How is the Bible study group going?"

"It's great," exclaimed Jeni. "I can read the Bible, pray and talk to others about things of the Lord. And Dee, I love singing the gospel songs."

"No one can appreciate that freedom more than you," Dee said.

After putting the phone down, Jeni broke into spontaneous song. "Amazing Grace. How sweet the sound, that saved a wretch like me." She lightly dropped herself onto the seat at her desk, and then Jeni put her faith onto paper.

*　　*　　*

New Life

A new light is shining
The darkness is gone
There's new life inside me
Through God's only Son.
The old sadness and sickness
Being taken away
Through the new life inside me
That Christ gave me one day.

He walked on this earth
And died on the cross
Jesus gave up His life
So mine wouldn't be lost.

His blood washed me clean
I'm no longer in sin
Since I opened my heart
And let Jesus come in.
He has healed my body
And made my mind sound
I have a new heart
Since my Savior I found.

I get stronger and stronger
With each passing day
Because Christ lives within me
And shows me the way.

I'm a child of God now
His love shines inside me
I've got a new life
Through Christ Jesus, I'm free.

Jeni

CHAPTER 14

Reflections

Remembering

Dee dropped into her recliner. Butch, the schnauzer, hastily joined his owner and settled down between the arm of the chair and Dee's hip. Dee's hand rested on the dog's back and she petted him a short while before she relaxed completely. She smiled as she remembered how he had yiped and jumped off the couch, ran to the far corner of the room and cowered when Dee rebuked the anti—Bible spirits. Even though she smiled now, it had been startling when it happened.

She mused as she remembered a particular Sunday morning. 'I'd like to make a prayer request,' she had told her students. 'Please continue to remember Jeni in your prayers for her total deliverance.'

'Dee,' Monica had spoken up, 'We prayed for her before. How come you're still asking for more prayer? After all, Jesus spoke one time and the demons left.'

My, what a startling comment, but I'm not Jesus, had been Dee's first thought. However, she had said to the class, 'She is better, praise the Lord! I suspect many demons have left, but there are still more.'

As her hand rested on Butch's back, Dee continued thinking of the changes in Jeni's life. She smiled gratefully toward heaven. "Praise you, Jesus, she is totally free now to worship you and live in obedience to you. She is now your loving servant, sharing you, Lord, and doing for others with joy in her heart." Dee was amused as she was reminded of Jeni's last phone call to her. With excitement in her voice, Jeni had told her, 'Dee, the ladies at the Bible study have nicknamed me Angel. Can you believe that?!? One woman told me that I am a real blessing and others agreed. Oh, what a difference in my life since Jesus came in and made me whole.'

Dee sat with her eyes unfocused. She pictured the Jeni she had first met and then pictured the Jeni who now exists. "Wow," she exclaimed out loud, "Lord, you are awesome!" The dog wagged his tail and looked up at Dee as if she'd spoken to him.

*   *   *

Forgiveness, Deserved or Not

Dee rocked gently for a few minutes in her rocker-recliner, then put the footrest up and closed her eyes. She could see the lovely, smiling face of Cindy, Jeni's mom. Dee marveled at Cindy's strong faith throughout the fourteen years of her daughter's mental illness. Cindy was a waitress at a truck stop where Dee serviced a rack of Christian books; they had been drawn to each other at that first meeting.

How horrible the revelation of repeated incest to her precious daughter had been, Dee thought. *I know Jesus said, 'But if you do not forgive men their sins, your Father will not forgive your sins', (Matthew 6:14) but this seems next to impossible. Yet Cindy persevered in prayer that the*

Lord would help her to forgive her father, until she was able to forgive him. In awe of this, Dee breathed, "Only you can perform that kind of miracle, Lord!"

Dee continued. "Jeni's anger toward her grandfather is understandable when one thinks of a small child being repeatedly hurt and unable to defend herself against this large person – when one thinks of the trust a small child has and the security needed from their beloved family members, and how that trust was utterly destroyed by Granddaddy's painful abuse and the threats he made to her to keep his behavior a secret.

"*No wonder* Jeni, like many other little tykes who were violated, tried to ease her pain by pretending she wasn't there." This is a mechanism used by others also, in an effort to handle such devastating circumstances. This is how and when Jeni's blank outs or amnesia began.

"*No wonder* Jeni was so bewildered during her childhood by accusations made of misbehavior, when she had no memory of misbehaving.

"*No wonder* so many well meaning and devout Christians gave up trying to help her. They did not recognize or understand what was behind the behavior during the blank outs.

"*No wonder* Jeni became so angry at Christians and the church. She had no idea why they dropped their efforts on her behalf."

"*No wonder* the results of the pattern of blank outs developed into utter hopelessness and anger towards all, cursing God and throwing her Bible. God had been her only hope and Jeni thought He had given up on her too, but He still loved her and guided her to the help she needed."

Dee nodded to herself. "Jeni wouldn't have made it back to God if she had not been willing to forgive all, who in her mind had hurt her. This included Granddaddy."

*   *   *

Demons: Fact or Fiction?

The ringing phone roused Dee from her reverie. "Dee, this is Jeni. Where is the scripture about the devil and his angels being thrown out of heaven?"

Dee reached for her Bible on the end table and opened it as she spoke. "That verse is found in Revelation, Chapter twelve, verse 9. I'll read it. 'The great dragon was hurled down – the ancient serpent called the devil, or Satan, who leads the whole world astray. He was hurled to the earth, and his angels with him.'"

"Dee, that says his angels. Why do we call them demons?"

"The word demon means 'evil spirit' in Greek," Dee replied.

"How did you know that I had some in me?"

"Well, Jeni, I read many missionary stories about them inhabiting people and my friend, Myrtle had some when I met her. What clued me into your problem with them was your strong reaction to the Bible; the wild fearful expression on your face, and the loud and angry demand that I not read it to you. I wondered then. When you went to sleep and the nightmares began with the contortions they put you through, I knew there were evil spirits within."

Jeni pursued, "How did you know when I was in control or blanked out, or when it was the evil spirits?"

"At first Jeni, I had to lean on the Holy Spirit completely to guide me, but I soon learned that you could not look at me when the demons were in control."

"One more question?" Jeni asked.

"Sure, go ahead."

"Maybe others dropped me because I acted angry and weird. Why didn't you tell me not to call you anymore?"

Dee chuckled with affection. "Dear Jeni, since you wanted this freedom in Christ so much, why should I deprive you of it? Jesus said to His disciples, 'Drive out demons . . . Freely you have received, freely give.' (Matthew 10:8). God through the Holy Spirit put you and your needs on my heart."

Jeni's own smile came through the telephone line. "Thanks, and now I can 'resist the devil' knowing 'he will flee' from me. (James 4:7) I've got that verse memorized, and I've digested the information in the prayer sandwich too. I start my prayers praising and honoring God like Jesus taught us in the Lord's prayer. Then I thank Him for all kinds of things: being saved, being able to read the Bible, being able to pray, and on and on. Then I state my problems and desires. Last of all, I pray for the church, His kingdom and God's power through the Holy Spirit and praise Him again for just being Himself."

"I'm so pleased, Jeni, at your diligence in learning scriptures and your obedience to them." Dee said.

"A Prayer Sandwich"

*   *   *

The Armor of God

Jeni continued. "There's something else, Dee, that I want to tell you about. The chart you gave me of the Christian soldier wearing the armor of God, I've put it above my sink. This is helping me memorize the different aspects of the armor, which I need."

"We all need it Jeni. I'm so pleased at your progress."

Enthusiastically, Jeni continued, "Let me see if I can name them all for you. The *helmet of Salvation*, the *sword of the Spirit*, which is the Word of God, Praying always . . ." Jeni paused.

Dee interjected, "I find that being aware of God's presence at all times and talking to Him throughout the day is a most helpful approach to prayer. I praise God for your helmet of Salvation, Jeni, and for the peace of mind it has brought you. It's also important not to neglect reading the Word of God. God talks to us through His Word, the Bible. Having God's Word in our minds allows the Spirit of God to teach and guide us."

"Hmm," Jeni pondered. "I'll have to remember that."

Dee pressed on. "Do you remember the other aspects of the armor of God?"

"Let's see, there is the *breastplate of righteousness*." Jeni went on to explain. "That means if I do what is right and don't do drugs, or sex until I'm married, or curse . . . If I read my Bible and pray and live as God would like, then I'm protected from old Satan and his fallen angels."

"Way to go Jeni," Dee encouraged and then challenged her further. "There are three more pieces of armor."

"Oh yes, peace . . . the *gospel of peace*. The news of Jesus and His salvation gave me peace. It also tells me I should try to live peaceably with everyone. The next one is *truth*. No more lies and deceit on my part, right?"

"Right," Dee agreed. "Now about the last one."

Jeni said, "I'm not sure I understand that one very well, but it's the *shield of faith*."

"A good start for understanding is found in Ephesians, Chapter 6, verse 16. 'In addition to all this, take up the shield of faith, with which you can extinguish all the flaming arrows of the evil one.' It is your faith in God and your obedience to Him that protects you from any more demon activity within."

"I get it! Oh, boy, I praise God for that shield of faith," Jeni exclaimed.

"There are two important things needed to keep your faith

strong. One is reading and listening to God's word, the Bible (Romans 10:17), and the other is a good prayer life. Without the armor of God, we couldn't have helped you, Jeni."

"Praise God for His armor," Jeni exclaimed. "I need to go, Dee, but I do want to thank you again. You really have been literally a godsend."

*   *   *

Ministering

Dee hung up the phone and slipped back into thought. *It has been difficult at times.* Dee sighed and thought of the unsaved adult son who had still been living at home. She did not rebuke demons when he was at home because of the story in Matthew 8: 28 through 32, where demons had gone from two people into a herd of swine. She had also read in a missionary's article on the subject to never have a deliverance service with children or unsaved present. There was a time, however, when her son John had come home during a rebuking session. Dee breathed a prayer, "Thank you, Lord, for protecting him at that time".

There were indeed times when it was difficult. John had been working on a degree in psychology at the time and often came home tired and drained. 'Mom,' he had said to Dee angrily at one point, 'I resent the disruption of my sleep by her noisy nightmares. Don't you realize with her diagnosis, that we might all be put into danger?' John's frustration and temper had been hard on her, but she smiled as she remembered his declaration of love and forgiveness to her at a later time. 'Mom, I know that you were trying to help her . . . and in fact did help her. I'm sorry I blew up at you.' Dee shed a tear at the memory, thankful for those precious moments. She was reminded of how much she had to be thankful for and once again offered praise to her living God and Savior.

Her thoughts turned to her own life. "I've been so blessed through the years, Lord. Thank you, for keeping me from straying in my teens to the spiritually dangerous and enticing elements.

Thank you, for guiding me not to date anyone that was not a devout Christian. Oh, praise your name for Harv. He is such a beautiful Christian. His love, patience and support of me is tremendous."

Harv had said to Dee several times, "I'm behind you with whatever God calls you to do," and he has been true to his word. His reassurances, his prayer support, his Christ-like opinions when Dee asked for them, all were such blessings. His willingness to be used of God was heartening, even though it sometimes made dents in the family finances.

"Thank you, thank you, thank you," Dee prayed, "for putting him in my life." Then she softly sang the chorus, "God is so good."

Yes Lord, her thoughts continued, *we are all called to go . . . and teach, just as you told us in Matthew 28: 19 and 20. How challenging and difficult it can be at times, when ministering to others.* She and Harv had been used to minister to relatively few people. "Lord," she prayed, "I can only imagine how overwhelming it must be for pastors, with so many folks calling on them for help because of sickness, sorrow, financial needs, emotional, marital and spiritual matters. Thank you, Lord, for pastors and their wives and their caring servant hearts.

"Jeni is free, totally free! Praise you, Jesus. You are faithful and good to deliver her from Satan's power. How marvelous that she is now your child, worshiping you freely, devouring your Word, praying regularly and telling others about you."

In her mind, Dee could hear Jeni's clear, vibrant soprano voice lifted in song as she had heard it not too long ago. Along with the young woman who now could live free in Christ, her own spirit soared and her voice joined in, singing and praising God with that favorite of Jeni's, "Amazing Grace".

PART TWO

SPIRITUAL WARRIORS

CHAPTER 15

New Testament Accounts of Demons

D ee acted as a Christian spiritual warrior in her confrontations with the demons which held Jeni in their grasp. She did march onward, as a Christian soldier. However, before a warrior can do battle, they must have an understanding of what and whom they are contending with.

Do demons even really exist? What does the Bible, and in particular the New Testament, have to say?

In Matthew, Jesus told his followers several parables, including the parable of the ten virgins and the one of the servants and the talent. Afterwards, he continued speaking of those who were righteous and those who were not. In Matthew 25:41, Jesus specifically states, "Then he [the King] will say to those on his left, 'Depart from me, you who are cursed, into the eternal fire prepared for the devil and his angels'." (All scriptures quoted are using the New International Version.) This is echoed in Revelation 12:9, "The great dragon was hurled down – that ancient serpent called the devil, or Satan, who leads the whole world astray. He was hurled to the earth, and his angels with him."

Note in both of these passages, the devil is specifically mentioned, but so too are his angels. So we can see that not only does the devil exist, but that he also does have fallen angels, or demons, who are under him, doing his malevolent bidding.

But could these and similar passages simply be speaking metaphorically? This supposition becomes less probable as one looks further into the scripture. The New Testament has several passages which describe demon possession in the same terms as other serious illness. Matthew 4:24 " News about him [Jesus] spread all over Syria, and people brought to him all who were ill with various diseases, those suffering severe pain, the demon-possessed, those having seizures, and the paralyzed, and he healed them." Some demonic manifestations will mimic physical afflictions, as can be seen in Luke 13:11 "And a woman was there who had been crippled by a spirit for eighteen years. She was bent over and could not straighten up at all." Mark and Luke both also report an incident that took place in Capernaum. Mark 1:23-26 "Just then a man in their synagogue who was possessed by an evil spirit cried out, 'What do you want with us, Jesus of Nazareth? Have you come to destroy us? I know who you are—the Holy One of God!'

"'Be quiet!' said Jesus sternly. 'Come out of him!' The evil spirit shook the man violently and came out of him with a shriek." Luke's account of this same incident, found in Luke 4:33-35, is very similar, stating that the demon threw the man down in front of everyone and then came out of the man without injuring him.

Another example of Jesus casting out a demon can be found in Matthew 15:22 & 28. "A Canaanite woman from that vicinity came to him, crying out, 'Lord, Son of David, have mercy on me! My daughter is suffering terribly from demon-possession." . . . . Then Jesus answered, 'Woman, you have great faith! Your request is granted.' And her daughter was healed from that very hour."

Certain demonic spirits are harder or more difficult to cast out than others. Mark 9:14-29 tells the story of a man who came to Christ asking for his son to be delivered from a demon which caused the boy to be mute as well as foaming at the mouth. The man had first met with some of Jesus' disciples, but they had been unable to cast out the demon. When he was brought to Jesus, the spirit threw the boy into convulsions. Jesus commanded the demon to leave him; when asked by his disciples why they had not been able to cast out the demon, Jesus replied to them that "this kind" can only be cast out through prayer, or only through prayer and fasting.

There are also situations in which several demons can inhabit one person. Such was the case written about in Mark 5:1-20. This passage tells of a man who was demon-possessed and who lived among the tombs, cutting himself with stones and crying out, and who had unnatural strength such that no one could restrain him, even with chains. When Jesus rebuked the demon and told it to leave the man, he shouted out at the top of his voice asking Jesus to swear not to torture him. Jesus then asked what his name was. The man replied, 'My name is Legion, for we are many.' The demons begged Jesus to give them permission to enter into a herd of pigs which were nearby. The herd numbered near 2,000 animals; upon leaving the man, the demons invaded the pigs and caused all of them to rush to their deaths in the Sea of Galilee.

*   *   *

As demonstrated in the passages above, as well as in other passages within the New Testament, demonic manifestations can take many forms. These manifestations include disruptive, violent and/or unmanageable behaviors, physical pain and/or crippling, muteness or deafness, self-mutilation, being placed into dangerous situations such as falling into water or fire, supernatural strength, and divination.

All of the above accounts concern Jesus directly confronting the demons. But was this something that only he could do? Or is there biblical support for the notion that believers in Christ are also able to command demons?

CHAPTER 16

Authority & Power Over Demons

J ust as there are a number of accounts of Jesus casting out
demons, there are also accounts of his disciples doing the
same. H ow is it that ordinary people became able to drive out evil
spirits?

In this, the metaphor of the Christian soldier continues to
parallel the world around us. Just like soldiers act on the authority
of their commanders, Christian soldiers act through the authority
granted them by their commander, Jesus Christ. This began with
the twelve apostles. Matthew, Mark and Luke report when Jesus
prepared and sent out the twelve disciples into the world. Luke
9:1, "When Jesus had called the Twelve together, he gave them
power and authority to drive out all demons and to cure diseases."
Mark 6:13, "'They drove out many demons and anointed sick

people with oil and healed them." Matthew 10:8 follows this same train; (Jesus speaking to the twelve) "Heal the sick, raise the dead, cleanse those who have leprosy, drive out demons. Freely you have received, freely give."

Was this just something granted only to the Twelve Apostles, though? No. Luke lets us know that this was not the case. Luke 9:49 & 50, "'Master,' said John, 'we saw a man driving out demons in your name and we tried to stop him, because he is not one of us.'

"'Do not stop him,' Jesus said, 'for whoever is not against you is for you.'" Luke also tells us that Jesus later sent out seventy-two believers. Luke 10:17 & 19, "The seventy-two returned with joy and said, 'Lord, even the demons submit to us in your name.' [And Jesus replied] 'I have given you authority to trample on snakes and scorpions and to overcome all the power of the enemy; nothing will harm you.'" Further, in Mark 16:17 we read, "And these signs will accompany those who believe: In my name they will drive out demons . . .". Paul and Silas later did just that, as recounted in Acts 16:16-19. They had been followed for days by a slave girl possessed of a spirit which told her the future. She kept shouting and causing a commotion everywhere they went. Finally, Paul turned to her and commanded the demon to leave her; it left immediately.

Even when things may seem overwhelming, Christian soldiers hold firm in their belief. The scripture tells us that when we are filled with the Holy Spirit, we will have power to do the work of God. Acts 1:8, (Jesus speaking) "'But you will receive power when the Holy Spirit comes on you; and you will be my witnesses in Jerusalem, and in all Judea and Samaria, and to the ends of the earth.'" As Philippians 1:27 & 28 says, "Whatever happens, conduct yourselves in a manner worthy of the gospel of Christ . . . . without being frightened in any way by those who oppose you. This is a sign to them that they will be destroyed, but that you will be saved – and that by God." Further on, in Philippians 4:13, Paul and Timothy write, "I can do everything through him who gives me strength." This admonition to be strong in courage through faith in the Lord is found throughout the Bible. Another such passage is Joshua 1:9, "Have I not commanded you? Be strong and courageous. Do not be terrified; do not be discouraged, for the Lord your God will be with you wherever you go".

*   *   *

Jesus Christ granted his followers the authority and the power over demonic spirits. As the soldiers of the faith, Christians can gather strength and courage, knowing and trusting in God's power and might. But is courage and faith enough when struggling against spiritual enemies? Or is there something more for the prudent soldier to know before heading off into battle?

CHAPTER 17

The Armor of God

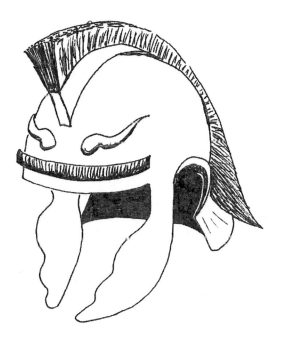

In his letter to the believers in Ephesus, Paul wrote a very detailed description of the spiritual armor of God. Ephesians 6:10-18, "Finally, be strong in the Lord and in his mighty power. Put on the full armor of God so that you can take your stand against the devil's schemes. For our struggle is not against flesh and blood, but against the rulers, against the authorities, against the powers of this dark world and against the spiritual forces of evil in the heavenly realms. Therefore put on the full armor of God, so that when the day of evil comes, you may be able to stand your ground, and after you have done everything, to stand. Stand firm then, with the belt of truth buckled around your waist, with the breastplate of righteousness in place, and with your feet fitted with the readiness that comes from the gospel of peace. In addition to all this, take up the shield of faith, with which you can extinguish all the flaming arrows of the evil one. Take the helmet of salvation and the sword of the Spirit, which is the word of God. And pray in the Spirit on all occasions with all kinds of prayers and requests. With this in mind, be alert and always keep on praying for all the saints."

This armor of the spirit is important to a Christian in dealing with the everyday ills of this world. How much more important it is to be properly gird up in the armor of God when dealing with and combating the forces of evil directly.

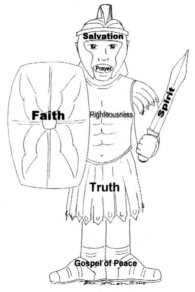

"The Armor of God"

*　　*　　*

The Belt of Truth

In terms of the armor of that day, the belt had a large number of strips hanging from it, generally of leather and occasionally reinforced with bronze plates. These belts protected the warrior from the waist to the mid-thigh; as such, they were very much a necessary part of the soldier's protection in battle.

Truth is just as necessary to the Christian warrior. There are a number of verses within the Bible to help the follower of Jesus focus their thoughts on truth. 2 Corinthians 4:2, "Rather, we have renounced secret and shameful ways; we do not use deception, nor do we distort the word of God. On the contrary, by setting forth the truth plainly we commend ourselves to every man's conscience in the sight of God." In John 8:31 & 32, "To the Jews who had believed him, Jesus said, 'If you hold to my teaching, you are really my disciples. Then you will know the truth, and the truth will set you free.'" John 14:6, "Jesus answered, 'I am the way and the truth and the life. No one comes to the Father except through me.'"

When strapping on the belt of truth, it is good to meditate and think on verses and passages such as these.

*   *   *

The Breastplate of Righteousness

The breastplate in physical armor protects the most important vitals a person has: their heart, their lungs, all of the organs in the torso. A Christian's spiritual breastplate must be strong enough to serve the same function. Any weaknesses here means that the Christian warrior is vulnerable to incredible damage to their spiritual self.

Here are several passages to consider and think on as one prepares mentally and spiritually to put on their breastplate of righteousness. Hebrews 12:11, "No discipline seems pleasant at the time, but painful. Later on, however, it produces a harvest of righteousness and peace for those who have been trained by it." 1 Corinthians 1:30, "It is because of him that you are in Christ Jesus, who has become for us wisdom from God – that is, our righteousness, holiness and redemption." 2 Corinthians 6: 4 & 7, "Rather, as servants of God we commend ourselves in every way: in great endurance; in troubles, hardships and distresses; . . . in truthful speech and in the power of God; with weapons of righteousness in the right hand and in the left." 1 Thessalonians 5:8, "But since we belong to the day, let us be self-controlled, putting on faith and love as a breastplate, and the hope of salvation as a helmet."

*   *   *

The Footgear of the Gospel of Peace

In order to stride confidently into spiritual battle, a Christian warrior needs to have their feet protected, not only from the attacks of foes, but also from the sheer rockiness of the terrain (the world we live in). Either one can cause the warrior to stumble; and that can have very bad consequences. Therefore, Paul tells us to enclose our feet in the gospel of peace; not acting out of anxiety or fear, but with full confidence and peace within ourselves. Other passages about peace include John 14: 27, where Jesus says, "'Peace I leave with you; my peace I give you. I do not give you as the world gives. Do not let your hearts be troubled and do not be afraid.'" In Philippians 4:6 & 7, we are told "Do not be anxious about anything, but in everything, by prayer and petition, with thanksgiving, present your requests to God. And the peace of God, which transcends all understanding, will guard your hearts and your minds in Christ Jesus." Hebrews 13:20 & 21 says, "May the God of peace . . . equip you with everything good for doing his will, and may he work in us what is pleasing to him, through Jesus Christ".

*   *   *

The Shield of Faith

When confronted by an enemy, the experienced warrior knows that often the best way to bear up under the barrage is simply to not allow it to hit them. That is what a shield is all about . . . stopping the weapon of the enemy from ever hitting them. Faith is the shield of the Christian fighter. In John 14:12, Jesus states, "'I tell you the truth, anyone who has faith in me will do what I have been doing. He will do even greater things than these, because I am going to the Father.'" One demonstration of this is found in Acts Chapter 3. Peter had healed a crippled beggar, then turned to the crowd. Acts 3:16, Peter says to them, "'By faith in the name of Jesus, this man whom you see and know was made strong. It is Jesus' name and the faith that comes through him that has given this complete healing to him, as you can all see.'" Faith includes the steady belief that God speaks the truth. There was a terrible storm as Paul was on shipboard in route to Rome. In Acts 27:25, he told the sailors, "'So keep up your courage, men, for I have faith in God that it will happen just as he told me.'" In Romans 3:25, we are told, "God presented him [Jesus] as a sacrifice of atonement, through faith in his blood . . ." and in Romans 10:8 & 10 we read, "But what does it say? 'The word is near you; it is in your mouth and in your heart,' that is, the word of faith we are proclaiming: . . . . For it is with your heart that you believe and are justified, and it is with your mouth that you confess and are saved."

*   *   *

The Helmet of Salvation

As we have just seen, faith and salvation fit very closely with each other. Without a head, there is no warrior. It is the one part of us that is the most important of all for our continued existence. It is no surprise, then, that the helmet of God's armor is made of salvation.

Here are several verses to think on in regards to salvation. Romans 1:16, "I am not ashamed of the gospel, because it is the power of God for the salvation of everyone who believes . . . ." Romans 6:2, " . . . We died to sin; how can we live in it any longer?" Hebrews 1:14, "Are not all angels ministering spirits sent to serve those who will inherit salvation?" Hebrews 5:9, "and, once made perfect, he [Jesus] became the source of eternal salvation for all who obey him . . . ." Revelation 12:10, " . . . Now have come the salvation and the power and the kingdom of our God, and the authority of his Christ . . . ."

*   *   *

The Sword of the Spirit

Lastly, we come to the only offense offered in God's armor. That is the Sword of the Spirit, which is the Word of God. There are many layers to this concept. As a beginning, think on the following verses. "In the beginning was the Word, and the Word was with God, and the Word was God." (John 1:1) Further on in John 15:7, we hear Jesus say, "'If you remain in me and my words remain in you, ask whatever you wish, and it will be given you.'" In John 17:17 Christ prays, "'Sanctify them by the truth; your word is truth.'" And in Acts 6:4, "[We] will give our attention to prayer and the ministry of the word." Finally, Paul says in 2 Corinthians 10:3-5, "For though we live in the world, we do not wage war as the world does. The weapons we fight with are not the weapons of the world. On the contrary, they have the divine power to demolish strongholds. We demolish arguments and every pretension that sets itself up against the knowledge of God, and we take captive every thought to make it obedient to Christ."

*   *   *

As you can see, every piece of armor fits and works in conjunction with every other piece. Faith without salvation is not enough. Nor can God's peace be found without righteousness and truth. The metaphor which Paul gave us concerning the armor and sword of God is as applicable now as it was then. And just as valuable to the Christian warrior, whether they are dealing with the everyday world or pitted against spiritual adversaries.

CHAPTER 18

Preparation of a Deliverance Team

"I keep asking that the God of our Lord Jesus Christ, the glorious Father, may give you the Spirit of wisdom and revelation, so that you may know him better. I pray also that the eyes of your heart may be enlightened in order that you may know the hope to which he has called you . . . and his incomparably great power for us who believe. That power is like the working of his mighty strength which he exerted in Christ when he raised him from the dead and seated him at his right hand in the heavenly realms, far above all rule and authority, power and dominion, and every title that can be given . . . . And God placed all things under his feet and appointed him to be head over everything for the church." (Ephesians 1:17-22)

*   *   *

The deliverance of a person who has been infested by one or more demons is not something to be considered lightly or carelessly. First and foremost, the person who is to be delivered needs to truly want to follow a Christian life. Jesus warns very specifically about the outcome if the one delivered from a demon does not fill themselves up with Godly things in Luke 11:24-26. "'When an evil spirit comes out of a man, it goes through arid places seeking rest and does not find it. Then it says, 'I will return to the house I left,' When it arrives, it finds the house swept clean and put in order. Then it goes and takes seven other spirits more wicked than itself, and they go in and live there. And the final condition of that man is worse than the first.'"

*   *   *

Examine Your Spiritual Life; You Must Be Born Again

Colossians 2:13 & 15 says to us, "When you were dead in your sins and in the uncircumcision of your sinful nature, God made you alive with Christ. He forgave us all our sins . . . And having disarmed the powers and authorities, he made a public spectacle of them, triumphing over them by the cross."

If your spiritual life is in order, you will be able to draw on God's power. **If not, however,** you are **not** in a position to attempt such direct confrontations of demonic entities. Unless you have given your life over to Jesus Christ, you are not protected by him nor do you have his power or authority.

*   *   *

Apply the Armor of God

Take up each piece of the armor, focusing your thoughts and meditations on each aspect. Examine yourself in light of each piece, looking for any breaks or chinks which need to be addressed before you go further.

*   *   *

Find and Read Scriptures on Deliverance From Demons

To go into a confrontation without having armed yourself with knowledge of your enemy is certainly not the wisest course. Be prepared. Think about the things which demons have been known to do, so that you won't be caught off-guard.

*   *   *

Pray for the Deliverance of the Candidate & the Protection of the Team

Prayer is like a spiritual power cord. Plug into the resources available to you as a Christian through prayer, asking God for his help and guidance, the deliverance of the candidate, as well as for protection for the candidate and the ministering team members. Everything and anything you have a concern about, pray about.

*   *   *

Fast as the Holy Spirit Leads

Some evil spirits are more tenacious than others; it is probable, given the scriptures, that sometimes those who are working to deliver another from a demon(s) will need to fast as a part of their preparations. Below are some passages concerning fasting.

(Jesus speaking) "'When you fast, do not look somber as the hypocrites do, for they disfigure their faces to show men they are fasting . . . . But when you fast, put oil on your head and wash your face, so that it will not be obvious to men that you are fasting, but only to your Father, who is unseen; and your Father, who sees what is done in secret, will reward you.'" (Matthew 6:16-18)

"While they were worshiping the Lord and fasting, the Holy Spirit said, 'Set apart for me Barnabas and Saul for the work to which I have called them." (Acts 13:2)

"Paul and Barnabas appointed elders for them in each church and, with prayer and fasting, committed them to the Lord, in whom they had put their trust." (Acts 14:23)

"Then John's disciples came and asked him [Jesus], 'How is it that we and the Pharisees fast, but your disciples do not fast?' Jesus answered, 'How can the guests of the bridegroom mourn while he is with them? The time will come when the bridegroom will be taken away from them; then they will fast.'" (Matthew 9: 14 & 15)

As with every undertaking, always pray for guidance, understanding and courage. As with every undertaking, remember that you are the representative of God, an emissary of light in a darkened world. Act only in accordance with His direction, not seeking to lift up your own self, but to lift up the work and power and salvation of Jesus Christ.

*   *   *

Jeni, as one who had lived under the dark influence of demonic spirits and found release from her bondage through Christ, knew first hand how terrible such bondage is. That is why she asked this book be written, to demonstrate that Christ is able to heal and deliver people from demonic bondage, that He has given his disciples the authority and power to also do so, and how His disciples need to approach freeing someone from such bondage. It is hoped that this book has given you, the reader, an awareness of the reality of demons, how to avoid opening the door to them, and how to be freed from them. It is also hoped that the work will be an inspiration and a testament to the reality of God and His joy and care for us.

For His is the power, and the glory, and the kingdom forever.

BIBLIOGRAPHY

Bounds, E.M.; *Winning the Invisible War* ; Whitaker House; Monroeville, PA; 1984.

Clark, Terri (M.D.); *More Than One* ; Thomas Nelson; Nashville, TN; 1993.

Hammond, Frank & Ida Mae; *Pigs in the Parlor*; Impact Books; Kirkwood, MO; 1973.

Jasson, Raphael; *The Challenging Counterfeit*; Logos Books; Plainfield, NJ; 1972.

Koch, Kurt; *Between Christ and Satan*; Kregel Publications; Grand Rapids, MI; 1962.

Michaelson, Johanna; *Beautiful Side of Evil*; Harvest House; Eugene, OR; 1982.

Olsen, Dr. Ken; *Exorcism: Fact or Fiction*; Thomas Nelson; Nashville, TN; 1992.

Peterson, Robert; *Are Demons for Real*; Moody Paperback; Chicago, IL; 1972.

Unknown Ed.; *Demon Experiences In Many Lands*; Moody Bible Institute; Chicago, IL; 1960.

Whyte, H.A. Maxwell; *A Manuel On Exorcism*; Whitaker House; Monroeville, PA; 1974.

Whyte, H.A. Maxwell ; *Dominion Over Demons*; Bonner Publishing; Monroeville, PA; 1973.

Whyte, H.A. Maxwell; *The Kiss of Satan*; Whitaker House; Monroeville, PA; 1973.

Wright, J. Stafford; *Christianity and the Occult*; Moody Paperback; Chicago, IL; 1972.

BVG